VIBRANT MEMORIES

Poems Of Whisper And Mystery That Bring Out The Vigour Of Heart

Gemma Escolano

Editor: Vincent Stead

Lismore, NSW Australia

Balboa Press books may be ordered through booksellers or by contacting:

Balboa Press
A Division of Hay House
1663 Liberty Drive
Bloomington, IN 47403
www.balboapress.com.au
1 (877) 407-4847

Mentor/Consultant: Voltaire B. Yabut
Visual Consultant: Lito C. Uyan
Senior Publishing Consultant: Jona Taylor
Publishing Consultant: Al Sampson
Publishing Service Associate: Rachel Abbey
Marketing Consultant: Pat Stone
Designer: Charisse Schelmer Hizon

ISBN: 978-1-5043-1982-9 (sc)
ISBN: 978-1-5043-1981-2 (e)

Print information available on the last page.

Balboa Press rev. date: 01/27/2020

BALBOA.PRESS
A DIVISION OF HAY HOUSE

ABOUT THE BOOK

This book is a collection of poems devoted to love poems and life in general. Every poem has different feelings of energy to convey the sometimes intense feelings of emotion of the writers to the reader, giving the perspective to look deeper at what is beyond love and the meaning of life that evolve constantly. They are mostly derived from the true stories and life experiences that have sunk and become embedded in subconscious levels of thinking. "A poem for me is a song from the heart and need to be heard, a quiet notes that only the heart can sing".

This is also a combination of my photography skills as a background in every poem. It shows the different places I went to, as one of my passions is to experience the beauty of Nature that gives relaxation and calmness to our senses.

ABOUT THE AUTHOR:

Gemma Escolano, a mother of five (5) beautiful lovely children and married to a loving husband, migrated with her family from the Philippines 14 years ago. With the support and guidance from her mum along the way of her career, she currently working in one of the prestigious Dental Practices in Sydney, Australia, the way of her career.

During her early childhood she grew up with a succession of different families, before finally meeting her father at the age of 14. At her young age, she started learning to earn from selling foods and other stuff for living. Lack of everything never stop her pursuing dreams, she tried many jobs and increased her knowledge by taking courses, all her life experiences bringing her courage and perseverance to chase her goals. From a young age, she wanted to do something to share what she can give.

Writing poems is her passion, therapy, way to express the emotions, feelings and life experiences of people, is part of her giving to the world.

Taking photos of interesting subjects, details, colours, events and Nature is her other passion. It gives the harmony of life, expresses the gratitude of all the blessings, the photos speaking silently of what you feel and express in all kind of situations. Loving the art of antique parquet specially, "tea sets" reminds those people's hands, how they are amazing moulding the intricate pieces of their small creations. The value of their effort, courage and perseverance….the essence of art.

Her passions has given Gemma the courage to pursue dreams, enlightenment and sharing with everyone, believing that like a million stars in the sky, there are ample of opportunities awaiting those being a part of this infinite Universe. Knowing and loving our inner-selves is the key to our happiness and success in life. Love starts within and spreads between one another to make the world a better place to live.

DEDICATION

This poetry book, "VIBRANT MEMORIES", is dedicated to my one and only lovely daughter, KIANA ESCOLANO YABUT, who is my pearl from the ocean abyss of my dreams and opened for me the window of opportunity to pursue my dream and bring this into reality. Who ignites the light within my heart, to share my thoughts, my passion, and love to everyone. Her vision has given me the courage to believe in myself that I can do things more than beyond my imagination. Thank you my sweet loving Duday for this amazing journey of my dream.

TABLE OF CONTENTS

"WINGS"

by: Gemma Escolano

Breeze around the place
Sunrise seems to be shown
Singing birds playing on the tree
Flower's blossoms, around the corner

What a beautiful day
That awakens my sleeping soul
Spreading the wings of dreams
Trying to fly high... Where to start?

Reaching the stars, touching the Moon
A dream that is longing for a time long ago
Fog and grey smoke blocking
The path that is waiting for me
Where is the avenue that is meant for me?

Energy of hope, passion and desire
Locked in a small, round, white cage
Released, come out, finding my way out
Like wings, finding a way
The window of my freedom.

Jalan Jalan Photography & Poetry
Gemma Escolano

ARTIST STATEMENT

WINGS

ABOUT THE POEM:

I wrote this poem on a quiet afternoon in early 2017, when an inspiration came to me about a soul wanting to be freed from the cage of own self, negative influences and the fear of the unknown. I grabbed a pen and paper, started writing what came into my mind about experiencing life beyond freedom and the things that could offer.

ABOUT THE IMAGE:

A bird flying around Huskisson beach February 2019. Huskisson is a suburb of Jervis Bay, New South Wales, where we spent a week holiday to celebrate my birthday.

"SHINING STAR"

by: Gemma Escolano

An endless dust that never counts
Shining brightly, as I look above
Colours seen that never fade
Through the thousand years, that have gone by

Like on Earth, countless grains of sand
The big wave came rolling in
Thrown by the giant sea
But no one can ever see

Modern world changes overnight
We're overruled by technology
People blinded by material world
Stress themselves to have it all

Beauty of the night they never felt
The shining stars they have never seen
Set their mind to what they want
To grab the things that never last

Essence of life they have never known
Message from above, they never heard
Forget the burden that brought the past
Embrace the present that you have had

Worry not for the future to come
Hold the brilliant stars that shine in you.

Jalan Jalan Photography & Poetry
Gemma Escolano

ARTIST STATEMENT

SHINING STAR.

ABOUT THE POEM:

I had a lot of things on my mind when I penned this poem. Now in the days of computer generation most people are busy juggling tasks one after another, meaning there is no time left for them to deal with personal things. In the stressful life of technology, sometimes we forget the best person that needs our attention…"Our own self"…that we have our own star within that needs to be cultivated and polished.

ABOUT THE IMAGE:

I took this photo of a big star on the top of our Christmas tree to represent this poem "Shining Star". My plan was to capture the night photo of stars in the sky but didn't happen because I don't have a good lens suited for night photography.

"YOU TOUCH MY HEART"

by: Gemma Escolano

You touch my heart when no one cares
Offer your hands with open arms
Lending your ears with sympathy
Walking with me with guidance way

You touch my heart, when dark time came
Giving me a candle to light me up
Showing the day with brighter tomorrow
Waking me up with promises of way

You touch my heart, when my tears falling down
Swept away my deep loneliness
Catching the moment to cheer me up
Laughing together with cheerful heart

You touch my heart, when you look at me
Showing your eyes with something to say
Giving your smile with your deep emotion
Say everything will be going fine

Your presence around is enough for me
Feeling with your sincere and genuine heart
With your loving care and tender thoughtfulness
With me is enough, because, you touch my heart.

ARTIST STATEMENT

YOU TOUCH MY HEART

ABOUT THE POEM:

Sometimes in our life, there's someone coming to you without out any expectation who helps you in some way, especially, when you are in the middle of hurdle in life. They are there to comfort you and help you to get through it. Giving security and lift you up to lighten what you carry. This poem is all about compassion and sympathy from a person who cares for you.

ABOUT THE IMAGE:

Taken this image in Mona Museum located at 655 Main Road, Berriedale, Tasmania, Australia. Hobart is the Capital City of Tasmania. The view was magnificent and you can see far away Mount Wellington in Hobart. I enjoyed every single day of my one week holiday in Hobart. My dream place to spend the rest of my life.

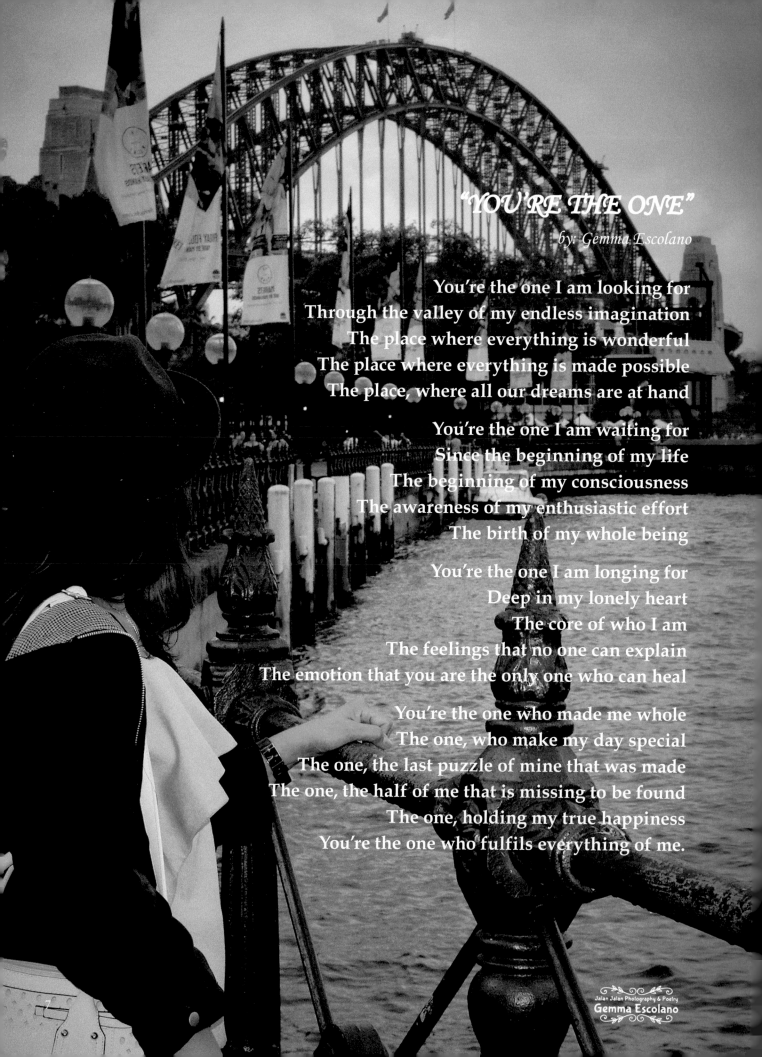

"YOU'RE THE ONE"

by: Gemma Escolano

You're the one I am looking for
Through the valley of my endless imagination
The place where everything is wonderful
The place where everything is made possible
The place, where all our dreams are at hand

You're the one I am waiting for
Since the beginning of my life
The beginning of my consciousness
The awareness of my enthusiastic effort
The birth of my whole being

You're the one I am longing for
Deep in my lonely heart
The core of who I am
The feelings that no one can explain
The emotion that you are the only one who can heal

You're the one who made me whole
The one, who make my day special
The one, the last puzzle of mine that was made
The one, the half of me that is missing to be found
The one, holding my true happiness
You're the one who fulfils everything of me.

Jalan Jalan Photography & Poetry
Gemma Escolano

ARTIST STATEMENT

YOU'RE THE ONE

ABOUT THE POEM:

We believe things happen for a reason, this poem is all about the person who is meant to be our partner in life. But before it happens, some people came to you that you think he or she is the one, but after knowing each other for some time, you have realized they are not the right one. Then afterwards the perfect match will come along your way. When this moment occurs, you know and feel that this person is the one match for you. Same energy, same chemistry, synchronised in many things and you are on the same page of the same feelings.

ABOUT THE IMAGE:

It was a lovely weekend, a beautiful day going around Circular Quay, Sydney Australia. I am passing through this Harbour Bridge everyday going to my work, seeing this wonderful City of Australia dreamt of by many.

"NO ONE LIKE YOU"

by: Gemma Escolano

Social media was fun
On the finger tips, shows me on
Far away, closer to you
Sharing thoughts, sharing fun

Pop on me, people depress
Giving words that hold their dreams
Show to them the way they take
Clear their minds, with smiling face

Many of you, asking myself
Begging for the contact to ease
I keep myself out, not to be judged
But I love my reserved self as I am about

Then you came into my chatroom
Surprisingly, your energy caught up on me
Conversations begin with a few bits of advice
Start with saying "Hello" until saying "Goodnight"

Excitingly, every day waiting for you
Visit my inside box that everyone can see
Your presence is a magnet that I can't explain
Knowing you're with me, makes my days precious

Unconsciously, I gave my contact to you
To know you more with curiosity in mind
Every day goes faster, easily, mingling with you
Having you near me enchants me

Among my proteges, you are one of a kind
Among my friends, you are the best
Among all the people I've known, you are different
Among the brilliant stones, you are the only gem
That mesmerized my vivid imagination

"No one is like you", as I always say to you
Something in your heart that never thought
That only true heart and good soul can feet
Coz, only in my heart, no one like you.

Jalan Jalan Photography & Poetry
Gemma Escolano

ARTIST STATEMENT

NO ONE LIKE YOU

ABOUT THE POEM:

We are created differently unique. We have our own talents, beliefs, life styles and are different in many ways. The thing that makes us different amongst all these unique persons is how you deal with your own life. How you use your given talent, communicate to others and what is your perspective in life and value to others. Being genuine and true by speaking from your heart, is what this poem is about.

ABOUT THE IMAGE:

This image taken in the suburb of Northbridge, NSW, Australia. I was standing on the street waiting to cross the road. That spot is close to the Northbridge and Cammeray Suspension Bridge.

"FEATHER"

by: Gemma Escolano

Fallen from the sky above
With my naked eyes surprise
With my deep thoughts of what I faced

Thinking of what the next will be
Looking for what is the answer behind,
he reason, the things that are needing to be done?

Signified hope, showed me instantly
fted up my spirit, from the dark cloudy time
Stressfulness faded away into the air
Changed the energy that worried me.

Someone out there looking at me
Guiding me to what I am to take
Showed me the sign, that I am not alone
In every step in my avenue of life

Every time, I ask the Heaven above
Sending me a sign to guess
Whatever it is, holding faith and courage
Believe everything will be aligned for us.

ARTIST STATEMENT

FEATHER

ABOUT THE POEM:

I wrote this poem through my experiences. There's a moment in our time when we don't know what to do when a problem arises, thinking so deep and looking for the answer. Despite my mind being occupied, I did notice that every time I am lost in my life journey, I saw a feather in front of me trying to catch my attention. I believe there are angels above who are watching and helping us, they are waiting for us to call them for help. The feather is a good sign for me, it answers the question of what I think is the best solution of my problem.

ABOUT THE IMAGE:

I photographed that feather hanging on the leaf of lemon grass in our backyard garden. That feather is one of my collection that I found manifested in front of me.

" THE BIRTH OF A RISING POET"

by: Gemma Escolano

The silent dragon in your heart
Sleeping in the dungeon of your soul
Slowly...slowly...slowly feels the urge to see the light
From the hidden ocean of silence darkness

Starting to spread the wings of desire
To fly and spread the vibrant light
From the abyss of forgotten memories
Trying to recall the world that it left behind
To feel the beauty of his creative mind

Step...step...small step to start
To start for the new world to see
To change the collective thought
From the wrong perspective of hungry mind

The beauty inside, hiding in your heart
Starts to glow the magnificent shine
The creation beneath, in your humbled soul
Starting to sing, the song of your heart and soul

Move...move...move the pen towards your dream
Dreaming of something wonderful to see
To let go the whispering dust of hope
To change the world into a better place

Here you are now, the birth of a rising Poet
Starting to spread the sprinkling pieces of your heart
To hear your soft magical voice of love
To touch the heart of every human mind.

Jalan Jalan Photography & Poetry
Gemma Escolano

ARTIST STATEMENT

THE BIRTH OF A RISING POET

ABOUT THE POEM:

This poetry is about my friend who is like a younger brother to me, from far away land of Europe. Who is also a Poet by nature. A down to earth kind hearted person, who is a very supportive friend. His masterpieces of poetry of love and the way he conveys emotions in the words touched me deeply through my heart. The unexplainable feelings of love offered to his loved one are so intense and magical. I can't see any person like him, the way he writes with the ingredients of truthful and honest love is so wonderful and fabulous beyond my imagination. This is the reason and where the inspiration came from when I write this poem that is dedicated only for him. I wrote this poem one morning on the train heading to my work and then wrote it on his birthday card that I was sent to him that day.

ABOUT THE IMAGE:

The background behind is my iPod that I bring where ever I go and is normally used to write my poems This represent that in this modern age, some poets use electronic devises for their writing. I added two (2) plastic flowers, peach and red wine colours of roses, to add beauty to the image. Underneath the flowers is the notebook that I bought from a book store in Tasmania during my short holiday a week in May of 2019. This notebook manufactured from "A Flame Tree Notebook" written on the back. The cover image is two (2) hands that trying to reach each other, to connect and to hold. This is the perfect matching image in this poetry. The connection of Heaven and Earth. On the top of the notebook is a feather to represent ancient time that used this as a pen to write. All the materials that I used in this image are synchronised with each other as a token of inspiration in our modern rising Poet.

"WHO AM I?"

by: Gemma Escolano

Asking myself with much thinking
Am I a grain of sand?
That ocean can give
Part of the big blocks
That build the houses and edifices

Am I a wood?
From the virgin forest
Part of the bush
Being cut by the loggers
Made of furniture, floors and everything

Am I a grass?
Growing in a wilder land
Harvested by the farmers
Feed for hungry cattle and horses

Am I a precious stone?
Part of the gem to be cherished
A glamorous lady in her majesty
That everyone adores

Am I a water to ease the thirst?
Giving life to everyone
From water falls running to the river
Heading to a giant ocean

Who really am I?
Am I giving sense in human race?
Or part of creation meant to be?
Or I am a humble one that no one cares...?

ARTIST STATEMENT

WHO AM I

ABOUT THE POEM:

This poem is all about our Earth Nature of how the Nature connected to people and the value of this Nature given to all on this Earth. Explaining how it is used and how to take care of this to benefit not only this generation but also the future of our planet Earth.

ABOUT THE IMAGE:

The golden colour of the grass and the background of blue colour river are perfect match that makes this image standout. Taken this image in the river of Hobart, Tasmania, Australia, during our trip with my Mum to celebrate her 75th birthday.

"YOU BRING BACK THE BEST OF ME"

by: Gemma Escolano

From the forest wilderness
You calling my name
Whispers to my ears
But I can't hear it clearly

From the top of the mountain
You waving at me
With your open arms
But I can't see it properly

From the valley of river
You talking to me
With your clear beautiful voice
But I can't listen attentively

Until the time it hit my heart
From the severe pain and agony
That dragged me into the dungeon
Of loneliness and emptiness

I can hear you now
I can see you now
I can give you now
My whole attention of me

Open my ears, the sounds of me
Open my eyes the beauty of me,
Understand the language
That only you, and I, can synchronise

Something within me, to come up
Something inside me, to give more
Something forcing me, to do more
Something covering me, the best of me
More than, beyond my imagination.

Jalan Jalan Photography & Poetry
Gemma Escolano

ARTIST STATEMENT

YOU BRING BACK THE BEST OF ME

ABOUT THE POEM:

Our life is so meaningful. We don't know where we are going or what we need to do and who is the 'we are' that belongs to us. Sometimes we felt loneliness, deep sadness and lost. Often we ask ourselves of what this life all about, but most of the time our minds are busy with many things and we forgot there is something within us that needs our attention and needs to become the best part of us. This is the inspiration that sits in my thought when I wrote this poem.

ABOUT THE IMAGE:

It was our 3rd day of stay in Riverfront Motel & Villas, Dr. Rosetta, located in the suburb of Tasmania. I ran outside from our room to catch this lovely sunrise, starting to show the Sun behind the mountain. The chilled breeze, the soothing atmosphere, the calmed water of the river and the singing birds flying around, was a magnificent and peaceful morning dawn. The Nature was so inviting to relax, thinking nothing and being in the moment. That's the reason I love Tasmania.

"BECAUSE OF YOU"

by: Gemma Escolano

I found myself to learn something new
Because of you
My existence being cultivated
By nature, by universe, by infinite

I found myself seeing the beauty of life
Because of you
Enjoying every moment of time
By sharing all my happiness and blessings I have

I found myself accepting the process of life
Because of you
Thinking the best time has not yet to come
By understanding, by patience, by knowing

I found myself helping others
Because of you
Sharing my knowledge, sharing my wisdom
By giving my hands with open arms
By loving them unconditionally

I found myself to caring and to loving myself
Because of you
Knowing my true self, the first step of happiness
Listening to the small voice deep within me
The guide, the instinct, the guts

It will never be a part from you
He is waiting, he is waving, he is listening
Knowing him, everything will be given to you
He made me a whole, a piece of creation
Because of you.

19

ARTIST STATEMENT

BECAUSE OF YOU

ABOUT THE POEM:

There is someone in our life that gives all the support that we need. Helping us to achieve our goals, helps us in many ways, the people behind our happiness and the people who bring the best of us, either a family, parents, partners, children or friends. They are there for us for a reason.

ABOUT THE IMAGE:

Taken this image on the top of the mountain of Mount Willington in Hobart, Tasmania. The formation and different sizes of the rocks so beautiful with the greenery of grass around. It was so windy and cold up there but slowly the Sun shows with warm rays.

"IN YOUR EYES"
by: Gemma Escolano

When I look into your eyes
I see myself, a mirror of me
Knowing myself better, who really I am
Finding myself further
Where I came from, where I am belonging.

When I look into your eyes
I feel the tranquillity
The peacefulness of my spirit
The awakening of my soul
A deep meaning of myself

When I look into your eyes
I sense the purity of your soul
The warmth of your energy
Wave of your magnetic field
Mesmerise myself up to a higher point

When I look into your eyes
Giving me the knowledge
That we are one, since Creation began
Scattered by galaxies from the infinite Universe.

Jalan Jalan Photography & Poetry
LITO C UYAN

ARTIST STATEMENT

IN YOUR EYES

ABOUT THE POEM:

This poem is part of Creation, our soul with the house of human body. As the old saying; "eyes are the windows to our soul"... the eyes cannot deny what are the feelings of body inside. The silent features that have a lot of meanings. You can feel what the energy is that the eyes can tell, mostly felt by people who are sensitive other's feeling. They easily catch what is the energy around when they look into their eyes.

ABOUT THE IMAGE:

It was my last day of short visit in Philippines, the morning of goodbye to everyone who are with me all the way during that time. A few hours before we went to the airport to go back home to Sydney. The house behind me, I called this; "Home of Dream and Beauty". I treasured every hour and single day of my stay in this place. Everyday there's something new coming up, a new thing to replace old things. The colours, the details and the textures in every corner of this home gives me happiness. Behind my smile is the mystery of wonderful dream. Don't give up, don't surrender, your dreams will be yours in time. This photograph took by; Lito C. Uyan, one of the best photographers and former Art Director from Manila, Philippines.

"I'M YOUR EVERYTHING"

by: Gemma Escolano

This is the line that you always say to me
That gives me smile on my cheek
That gives me joy in my heart
That gives me delight in my soul

But, still wondering, if you are truly the one?
Coz, I haven't seen you yet, in front of my eyes
But you always assure me, saying that,
"You are the one, you can't tell,
But I can prove it to you."

Every time you are whispering words
Sounds a melody, of a song for me
That swings me into the air of happiness
That brings me the glee that shines from far away

Every time you are remembering me
You always say the words that sound like; a poem for me
The remarkable, a noble poet from a distance
A poet of all generations, that is never forgotten

Sometimes, you missed a second of moment
Coz of your unavoidable way of sourcing a living
But you fill the time, with your romantic loving words
That bring back again, my enchanted sweet smile

You want me to be happy all the time
With eloquent beam of radiant joy
That comes out from my innermost
That bring your spirit dancing with love of happiness

But, my words for you, repeatedly,
"When the right time comes, I can tell and feel,
If you are the one, when you are in front of me
Telling me this..."I'm you're everything".

Jalan Jalan Photography & Poetry
Gemma Escolano

ARTIST STATEMENT

I'M YOUR EVERYTHING

ABOUT THE POEM:

This is all about the guy who offers his love to the woman he adores. The line; "I'm Your Everything" are the words he is always whispering to the woman. But it's hard to believe if this guy is true in his feelings of love until he proves and reveals himself and she sees him personally. This story gave me inspiration to write this poem.

ABOUT THE IMAGE:

It was a night before my brother's wedding (first Saturday of November 2019). We arrived at the location for the wedding at EL Pablo Resort Swimming pool located at Montevideo Subdivision, Brgy, Binangonan, Rizal, Philippines. My attention was caught by this big tree in the middle of this place that was full of hanging lamps. A circular shape made of capiz shell covering the valve that gives these lights the look of elegant, vintage and yet are native, traditional. Capiz shell is from a marine mollusc originally from the coastal waters of Capiz town in Visayan Region in Philippines. This province is well known as the "Seafood Capital of the Philippines". There's a lot of things can be made from these beautiful sea shell, like chandeliers, jewellery, plates, pendant lights, lamps, vases and Christmas decorations. Even windows and doors from old native house in Philippines most of them are made of capiz.

"WAITING FOR YOU"

by: Gemma Escolano

"Waiting for you", the last word I say
Seeing you walk away from me
Going back to your familiar place
To prepare something new to see

Waiting for you, just remember
Our precious time together
Day and night knowing us
Holding deeply within us

Waiting for you, thinking of me
Sharing our thoughts
Knowledge and wisdom
Our reunion unexplainable

Waiting for you, bear with me
You will return, promise me
Longing for you, please stay with me
Piece of your heart, you will find in me.

ARTIST STATEMENT

WAITING FOR YOU

ABOUT THE POEM:

The love story of lovers, one is left and one is waiting. Sometimes love cannot explain the way it is. Just go with the flow and embrace the process. We never know what our love relation could be after all the wonderful moments and trials along the way. The only thing we can hold on is hope, hope that one day the love that meant for us shall be returned.

ABOUT THE IMAGE:

It was me sitting on the lounge lobby in the hotel of Sea Residences Condo, located at Sunrise Drive corner Pearl Road, Mall of Asia Complex, Pasay City, Philippines. My first night of a short holiday, early November of 2019. It was a lovely night after we had a beautiful dinner with my cousins and very close friends. The ambiance of the place is warming and inviting to have some pictures around the area. The most important thing at that moment is not the food nor the place, but the time that I met my long lost friends after more than two (2) decades. They are one of those lovely persons who gave me a chance to prove and believe to myself that I can pursue my dreams and do something wonderful to share to others. It was Lito C. Uyan who took my picture.

"MAGICAL CONNECTION"

by: Gemma Escolano

Somewhere deep inside me
Wanting to come out
Intense feelings, no one can explain
What is this all about?

A series of numbers 11:11
A feather along my way
A coin from the stairway
A butterfly soaring around me

Is this a sign from Universe?
Something magical happens
I can't resist the energy flowing
Something odd, something strange

Until the day I met you
Like, descending from above
Blowing my mind away
Can't imagine, that moment of day

Is this what "Twin Flames" is all about?
Feeling have been together, long time ago
Knowing each other from the past
A familiar face, that we never forget.

27

ARTIST STATEMENT

MAGICAL CONNECTION

ABOUT THE POEM:

This is about the unfamiliar feelings that we cannot explain in words. Some sort of something that is hard to express. There will be time in our life that we think the person we met or event that lookS familiar, or things happens before, but we don't know who, when or how?

ABOUT THE IMAGE:

This image taken 2017. My family and I had short jalan-jalan for a day at Wollongong beach, NSW Australia.

"YOU ARE MY PRINCE"

by: Gemma Escolano

Standing in front of a big, iron gate
Waiting for you, waving at you
Returning home from long journey
From a foreign land far, far away.

Here you are, standing in front of me
Seeing you again with my naked eyes
Staring at me, you're deep loving eyes
An angelical face, with cry full of excitement.

You embraced me without saying a word
So tightly and lovingly intimate
Saying words that are hard to express
The happiness lying within your faithful heart

I felt the warmth of your presence
I heard every beat of your heart
Our energy synchronised together
That departed long, long time ago

The love that binding us together
No one can explain, no one can believe
Let the hearts talk and express
And feel the love, of energy that we have shared

And then now you are with me
There's no point leaving me again
My long wait, longing for you
Will be ended, this journey of life

You are the meaning of my life
You are the lyrics of my songs
You are the last piece of my puzzle
In my heart, in my mind, soul and spirit
You always be my Prince for life and forever.

Jalan Jalan Photography & Poetry
Gemma Escolano

ARTIST STATEMENT

YOU ARE MY PRINCE

ABOUT THE POEM:

The idea of a handsome Prince derives from many books of fairy tales, this thought comes first into my mind when I wrote this poem. The right perfect match Prince on their own that waiting for so long. This love story down to generation after generation. Different persons but the story itself was the same.

ABOUT THE IMAGE:

I took this photo of bridge located in the suburb of Northbridge on the lower north Shore of Sydney, Australia. This is under the local government area of Willoughby and linking to the suburb of Cammeray. They call this bridge, "The Suspension Bridge". Build and completed in January 1892, recognised as the icon of Northbridge. This place is close to my work, about 10minutes walk away. Every time I'm passing through this, it's like, I am entering the passage going to the castle, as this structure like the time of Medieval era. I was amazed at the beauty of this architectural design.

"I FOUND YOU"

by: Gemma Escolano

My long journey of searching for you
Longing for your loving heart
The warmth of your tender touch
The sweetness of your loving voice

The pain inside my heart
From the time that you're not mine
The emptiness settling in my life
Hovering in the cold and lonely nights

Each and every day passes with emptiness in my heart
Always grey and dull, lifeless and weak
Every tick of the clock is meaningless to me
Every corner of my site was colourless to me

Here you are now, the reality of my dreams
From my sweet deep sound sleep
Waking up this time that you are already mine
In my heart, in my soul, in my spirit and in my life

My life transforms into brilliant days
My heart beats more normally than before
Every beat saying, I love you so much
I have never felt so much happiness

Now, I found you, the best part of my life
I don't want you to leave me again
Please hold me tight, hold my hand, hold my heart, hold my soul
Walk with me all the way on our journey of happiness
The love that binds us together, will never come apart.

ARTIST STATEMENT

I FOUND YOU

ABOUT THE POEM:

The love story that waiting and longing for many years. Finally the waiting is over. The deepest love for someone, the sing of the heart. When we are a child growing up into an adult, we learned from our parents and relatives to love and care to one another, but deep in our heart there is something missing, some space that needs to filled. That could be the love that we are waiting for when the right time comes when we are ready to merge into one.

ABOUT THE IMAGE:

It was a lovely day, the white smooth sand, the blue water of sea, the soothing wind are perfect to have stroll by the beach. The place is in Huskisson, Jervis Bay, NSW Australia.

"YOUR PRESENCE IS JUST ENOUGH"

by: Gemma Escolano

To be with you is magical
Like the air snatching my breath away
Keeping me alive for you to love
I can't live without you in my heart

Feeling you're with me is enough
For each and everyday full of countless happiness
Sharing our thoughts, sharing our floss
Can't help showing how much you mean to me

Knowing you're with me is a blessing for me
Fixing things that haven't been done like that before
When you are not yet by my side
Can't do anything without you in my life

Thinking of you is feeling wonderful
Like everything in every way, full of beauties
No words can comprehend, no action can portray
Can't think properly, without you there guiding me

Holding you in my arms is my greatest fulfilment
Like the rhythm of my songs in every beat of my heart
Let us walk together on our journey of eternal love
Coz, just your presence is enough for me to live.

Jalan Jalan Photography & Poetry
Gemma Escolano

ARTIST STATEMENT

YOUR PRESENCE IS JUST ENOUGH

ABOUT THE POEM:

If we love someone, we devote our time, we give effort to do something for them to be happy. The happiness is what we felt even in small things when we are with them. They give us strength, perseverance and inspiration for us to grow and develop our own capacity to do more of something better for ourselves and love ones, that's why the presence is just enough.

ABOUT THE IMAGE:

I took this lovely purple orchid flower from Bunning shop close to my place. Flowers signifies many things like; happiness, strength and hope. Flowers are one of my favourite things to photograph.

"GOODBYE MY LOVE"

by: Gemma Escolano

Hard to say goodbye to you
But this is the only word that I can say to you
After all the happiness and tears with you all along
A big step in my life that I have to do

Letting you go away from my life
Broken pieces of my heart that scattered away
The memories that are settling on my mind
They never leave, they never fade

In your deepest heart, you have always known
How hard I really tried to make us work things well & good
But the time for us doesn't agree
Doesn't fit, doesn't go well

Many decades I kept you in my heart
We had sometimes been away for quite a long time
Until the day I saw you again
The fulfilment of my desire, to be with you again

But now, with the tears of blood from my heart
Hard to say goodbye, but I have to do it
For you to move on to what is meant for you
For me to wait for what happiness that belongs to me

Always remember after all those memories
You're always in my heart, will be no matter what
Coz you are the one who showed me the meaning of love
But our time is ended, so time to face our different life

Goodbye my love.....goodbye my love....
Be strong, be brave, be tough
Without me in your life, you will be fine
Until we meet again in other time.

Jalan Jalan Photography & Poetry
Gemma Escolano

ARTIST STATEMENT

GOODBYE MY LOVE

ABOUT THE POEM:

I remember this love story. About the teenage lovers that deeply-love one another, but as time went by, they separated due to unexpected situation. The girl continued thinking of her first love because they were separated accidentally without saying goodbye to each other. She's waiting and hoping that someday their paths would cross again… but in the end they remain separated.

ABOUT THE IMAGE:

During our stay in Hobart, Tasmania, Australia, the colour of morning sun was different every day. Before the Sun started to rise, I get up early to catch this beautiful dawn. The serenity of water and cold of breeze were energising my body and relaxing my mind. The singing birds flying across the river was like music humming in my ears. Living closer to water is more beneficial for health being. The natural water from river release the invisible molecules called negative ions that produce positive energy that alleviates depression and relieves stress. The reason most people living near water are happier and stress free. Across the river on the left hand side is the Mona Museum of Old and New Art, the largest privately funded Museum in the Southern Hemisphere.

"I SEE YOU IN MY DREAM"

by: Gemma Escolano

Walking together on a sea shoreline
Catching the wave with footprints in the sand
A beautiful morning, sunrise to see
What a miracle, a day with you my lovely sweet

Holding hands together while counting the foot steps
Feeling the smooth sands, the water pushing
With smile on my face, the breeze touching with enchanted wind
What a marvellous time, feeling light, feeling blessed

Hearing together the singing birds flying closer to us
Matching of the waves sounds rushing towards us
With the cold winds whispering in our ears
What a magical moment that we can't imagine

If this is only a dream, I don't want to wake up
My desire of having you, the core of my happiness
I rather sleep with you forever,
Than waking up, without you by my side
You are my missing half, my eternal, my forever love

But I see you in my dream, we're sitting together on the beach
Watching the sunset, slowly hiding from the sea
You holding me tight, warm and secured
Telling me, we always be together every beat of our hearts.

ARTIST STATEMENT

I SEE YOU IN MY DREAM

ABOUT THE POEM:

This poem is all about the love that one is waiting for. Even in the dreams is manifesting the love that set in the core of heart. Because these feelings continuously thought of by the mind and felt in the heart, will bring them into a dream that the subconscious minds remind the body to feel this.

ABOUT THE IMAGE:

Taken this image at Jervis Bay, NSW Australia. I'm just walking by the beach and felt the water rolling to my feet, the smooth sand touching my skin, and the warmth of rays of Sun, everything is just like, perfectly magical.

"HERE COMES THE MOMENT"

by: Gemma Escolano

Walking in the aisle of my eternal happiness
Wearing stunning long white gown
With the beads of love that never fade
Dressed with marvellous laces around the hem

The long veil covers my face, hiding my tears of joy
The purity of love, like the white dress I am wearing
The long white smooth silk of trail, shining with stones
Shielding me from the unbelievable look from the eyes of many

Beautiful, long, thick, red carpet along my way
Colour of my heart belongs to my Prince
Greenery and white of roses and flowers, placed side by side
Signifies the beauty and deep feelings inside me

In every step closer to you
I leave behind the memories of past
The loneliness hovering around me, the abyss of my emptiness
The heartaches, the unwanted, the frustrations

Here comes the moment of my dreams
Holding in my hand, one step away
Dreams awaited for so long, years passed by
Now in front of me, the reality of blissful moment

Waiting for me at the end of my journey
For us to have a beautiful and happy life together
Staring at me with your sweet and loving smile
The love you give me, unexplainable, immeasurable

Now, we are facing in front of the Divine Almighty
Lovingly sharing vows sincerely with each other
The unbreakable promises that no one can interfere with,
No one can oppose, no one can conquer

The tie that binds us together will never break, will never loosen
In front of our relatives, friends and colleagues
Praying and wishing us, our love will never end
The promise that I always give to you faithfully
My life, my breath, my heart, will always belong to you.

Jalan Jalan Photography & Poetry
Gemma Escolano

ARTIST STATEMENT

HERE COMES THE MOMENT

ABOUT THE POEM:

This is the dream that most ladies are dreaming of. The wedding to be remembered for life time. Sharing the love for the man of their dream for the rest of their life. When I wrote this poem, the inspiration that came to me was the story of a famous fairy tale Rapunzel. The famous fairy tale love story of all generations. Rapunzel is my most favourite among of the fairy tale characters. How her life struggled on the early time and she dream that someday, a Prince would come to rescue her. Take them out from the place of loneliness and emptiness.

ABOUT THE IMAGE:

Took the photo from our backyard. It was lovely afternoon, thinking of what is the best shot I give on this poem. I used my two (2) rings to signify the wedding bond. I can't find any rose flowers or some flowers to these. Instead, I used the other plant that my mum planted. It is the green leaves of what we called; 'oregano'. This plant is herbal medicine and also the leaves used as garnish for some delicious food. The juice of this plant is very good to heal the cough.

"KNOWING YOU LOVE ME IS ENOUGH FOR ME"

by: Gemma Escolano

We've been good friends since we met
Open to you is what is deep inside me
Giving me wisdom that only you can understand
Giving me your time that only you can share with me

The burden inside me, the heavy loads I carry
Everyday getting faster and lighter to me
Every step on my way, you're guiding me
Every dream of my own, you're cheering me

You're calling me a shining star
That's what you feel and see, about me
You place me in a right spot, as you look at me
Even in the dark moments, shines are seen beneath of me

When I look at you, I felt like, I have known you long time ago
You're so close to me, feeling what I can't understand
Time passes quickly, we do not notice
Slowly, every day you feel something special about me

Until the day the feelings manifest
Get up to the surface of reality that you can't resist
Surprisingly, with your sincere deep looking eyes
I feel and grasp the energy around what you are holding on to

The feelings same as with me, but maybe in different way
With our age gap, can't be together as one
With our different beliefs, can't be merged into one
All I can say is, I am thankful our path crossed
Knowing you love me, is enough for me.

Jalan Jalan Photography & Poetry
Gemma Escolano

ARTIST STATEMENT

KNOWING YOU LOVE ME IS ENOUGH FOR ME

ABOUT THE POEM:

This is about a friend who turns into a lover. He always there to help in everything that he can offer, a shoulder to cry on and the ear to listen of all the stories she has to tell. But they are totally different when it comes the age, religion, culture and believe. The love of this friend remains until the end, and that is what the poem is all about.

ABOUT THE IMAGE:

It was early morning around 6am, we rushed outside to catch this lovely morning before having our breakfast. The magnificent Sun slowly came out from behind the mountain. The water in the river was so calm and peaceful. I heard the birds flying and singing around, like; greetings and welcoming us to this magnificent Nature. When I took this image, it was my mum on the background, busy on her own.

"A CHILD'S WHISPER"

by: *Gemma Escolano*

Someone out there, someone is longing for
A child that has grown up lacking motherly love
Lonely nights, freezing nights, tears on his cheek
Where are you Mum?...I've been waiting for you

An angelic face, an innocent look
A beautiful soul, has loss of a motherly care
You always whispering, someday coming to you
A loving mother that you are longing for

Many times in your life, you live by yourself
Only friends, classmates, are always around you
Accompanying them, is enough for you
To end the day, with laughter, and cheerful times together

But deep in your heart, there's emptiness
How would be the feelings, if my mum is with me?
How would I be with my mum's thoughtful and tender care?
How would my life be, every time you're around me?

I wish, you would be here when I needed you most
Hugging me and comforting me, when I'm scared
Telling me a story, before I go to sleep
Kissing me goodnight, with your sweet loving smile

I wish you will be here, when I perform at school
Cheering me, encouraging me, to give my very best
Proud of me, among, with other kids
Happy for me, of what I am now

I know, somewhere, somehow, I will find you
The best day ever, in my whole empty life
Hugging and kissing you, is what I wanted to do
Wishing that someday soon we will meet.

Jalan Jalan Photography & Poetry
Gemma Escolano

ARTIST STATEMENT

A CHILD'S WHISPER

ABOUT THE POEM:

I remember this story of a boy who was alone, left by his mum at the age of 4. The feeling of longing for love of this boy inspired me to write this poem. The emotional feeling of loneliness and deep sadness that brought to him being strong and brave to keep going in life. Only hope in his heart that someday they will reunited.

ABOUT THE IMAGE:

It was my youngest son's photo when he was 10 year old. Taken early 2018 in Hawkesbury River located in central coast, New South Wales, Australia. To get there catch the train from City Central Station going to New Castle then get off in Hawkesbury River train station for stroll by the park near the water.

"A MAN OF BEAUTY AND FAME"

by: Gemma Escolano

The smile on your face, telling story
How great you are, how wonderful you are
Someone who trusted too, someone to rely on too
The smile to connect everyone, straight from your heart

The knowledge that you carry
Given by Almighty, born to you, meant for you
You are chosen to heal the world
To open their mind to infinite reality

With your hand with the magic touch
You heal the body, mind and soul
Every time you perform on the platform of life and courage
A magical happens, a new hope, a new life in every sick patient

With your passion, create the dreams of many
The living example for anyone that is paying off
Achieving their goal one touch ahead
To reach the end of their marvellous success

The love you shared, melting the hearts of many
The true, honest, sincere and magnificent fellow
The beauty of your soul and the serenity of your spirit
Has given courage, hope and happiness to each & everyone

The energy that you possess, gives a light to the world
To live their life into wonderful, fruitful and abundance
To remind everyone how blessed we are
From the beginning of our human race
Coz we are the infinite creation,
a birth that has right to be happy.

Jalan Jalan Photography & Poetry
Gemma Escolano

ARTIST STATEMENT

A MAN OF BEAUTY AND FAME

ABOUT THE POEM:

This poem is dedicated to all the wonderful doctors of our time. The dedication, love, sincerity and passion to help and serve people, inspired me to write the unforgettable words that they deserved and leave a memories of all time.

ABOUT THE IMAGE:

I used stethoscope to represent as connected with this poem about the doctors. I used my D7000 Nikon Camera with the lens AF-S Nikkor 85mm 1:1.8G. The focus was brilliant. I always use this lens for the better result of my subject.

"I WANT YOU TO KNOW"

by: Gemma Escolano

I want you to know, I am here with you
Always thinking, remembering you
Never forgetting you nor losing you
My thought, my heart, saying only your name

Even though we're far apart
Miles and miles away
But my time closer to you
Always near, always with you

Those happy days, flashing all the way
Treasured times, always make our way
You gave me a wonderful moment
That lasts forever, confining my heart and mind

You stand with me through my rough days
Until it clear and brightly sunny days
You walk with me down my rough & winding road
Until it was smooth and straight light road

You holding me in my vulnerable feelings
Showing me, it will be gone, it will be fine
Hugging me saying, I am always here
Telling me, everything will be wonderful time

Every moment, I close my eyes
I see your loving face, smiling, staring at me
I feel you in my heart, the warmth and tender love
I touch you in my dream, hugged tightly and feeling secured

My hope and prayer, someday, somehow
I will see you again, thanking you
For all the things you shared with me
For all the moments you gave me
For all the faithful love you showed me
Coz, all those memories were part of you and me.

ARTIST STATEMENT

I WANT YOU TO KNOW

ABOUT THE POEM:

Somewhere, along the road, we can met people who give us special time, who open our eyes to know ourselves and bring out the best of us. Who shows respect and honesty, the person of love and passion, a down to earth soul and beautiful spirit. The memories of someone, inspired me to write this poem. The time of never ending memories. The precious time of all seasons. Thank you for all those times.

ABOUT THE IMAGE:

I love this image so much. The jetty on the river side, a better place to have your moment, catching the wind, watching the sunrise, the serenity of the water, the calm and peaceful place. Think nothing and free your mind. Fly your spirit of imagination into the place of happiness. This place is the river at the suburb of Dr Rosetta located in Tasmania, Australia.

"PETALS OF LOVE"

by: Gemma Escolano

Lying in a cold, white single bed
With all the machines attached to you
Helping you add to your days, but killing me softly
Time is running out quickly, and I'm in pain

I heard your voice whispering
Slowly coming to my ears constantly
A deep and soft voice, like, from a cave
I can't hear it loud and clear

You want to say something
Struggling to speak up properly
I felt in my heart, I'm afraid
I know, this is the last word you can speak

I hold you in my arms so tight and warmth
Closer to my heart, closer to me
I want to feel you, for the last time
I know.., I know…. Your time nearly ends

My heart starts beating faster, broken inside
Like, falling glass, scattered everywhere
Tears of blood flowing from my heart
Spikes of thorns, go deeper into my heart

I feel cold, like, a bucket of iced water
Thrown and pouring within me
Freezing, like, in the middle of Winter
I feel hot, boiling inside, like, Summer time
Like, in the middle of blazing bush fire
No, where to go, no, where to escape

But I want to hide these feelings from you
I don't want you to see, I am in so much pain inside
But my body is shivering holding these feelings from you
I want you to see me, cheerful and happy, like before

I won't let you go, I won't see you go
I want to give you, the best of everything
I want to spend the rest of my life with you
My love, I want to hold you in my arms forever
Where ever you go… please… bring my heart with you.

Jalan Jalan Photography & Poetry
Gemma Escolano

ARTIST STATEMENT

PETALS OF LOVE

ABOUT THE POEM:

One of my colleagues at work told me about her friend's wife who was dying. I was deeply touched by all the words she spoke. How her friend handled the last moment of his wife who was sick and struggling of cancer for a long time. The pain and the sadness was so intense, and I could not help myself crying. This unfold story inspired me to write this poem in honour of my colleague's friend's wife.

ABOUT THE IMAGE:

I used my summer hat with the bouquet of greenery flowers to signify the love of departed loved one. The photo taken at our backyard in the middle of morning while the Sun is up to give the perfect light to my subject.

WHAT SHOULD I DO?"

by: Gemma Escolano

Question thrown into the air
Finding the right moment to hear
After I heard, the words from you
Your heart, speaking sincerely, out of you

Sending to the Universe the mixed up thought
Seeking the answer, of what I need to do?
Blowing my mind away, of what you want to do
Giving your feelings, that you can't hold on to

"I want to be with you, for the rest of my life
I want to take care of you, each and everyday
I want to give you what you really like
I want to give you, my faithful love, only for you"

Those words, gave me a lot of thoughts
What should I do? My response to you
Are these feelings true, or only impulsive?
Is your heart sincere, or are you only blind?

Blind to what is the real world in which we are walking
Deaf to what others may say or be thinking
Frozen as to what is the action you are taking?
Speechless as to what were the right words were saying?

Knowing our large age gap, you don't care
Knowing our different religious belief, you say, "It doesn't matter"
Knowing our different culture, your response, "It's not the problem"
Knowing our long distance gap, you only say, "It can be sorted"

Telling you all the hindrance of all these feelings
Trying to open your mind to what it is all about
"Love is all that matters", that's all your responses
"My life is to be with you, the only time, I want to have"

ARTIST STATEMENT

WHAT SHOULD I DO

ABOUT THE POEM:

This poem is about the guy who developed feelings for a woman older than him. In spite of lots of differences between them the guy continues loving this woman, but this woman wondering and doubting if this guy's feeling is true love or only infatuation that overwhelms him from this woman's kind-hearted and sweet friendly approach.

ABOUT THE IMAGE:

On that early morning, the Sun starting to show with a brilliant colours mix of red, orange and yellow. The transformation of colour from black of night to the bright morning day. The colours reflection on the water river that gives a peaceful harmony on that place of Rosetta, the suburb of Tasmania, Australia. At that moment of time, I felt the happiness inside, like free of everything. Freeing my mind and soul, relaxing my body to catch the momentum of Nature.

"IHSAN"

by: Gemma Escolano

You came from nowhere
In the midst of my loneliness
Without expectation, without any hint
My confusing thoughts fog into darkness
Questions behind, trace with no response

A longing for deep in my heart
Stay for so long, need to be known
Emptiness of my soul lost at dawn
Waiting for sympathy and a warmth embrace

You are an angel, light my pathway
Every step along the way
Every teardrop in my eyes you wiped away
For me to show my smile again
You sail the boat away from stormy sea
Through the rough waves and thunderstorms foresee

You are the star in the middle of the night
Shining above in the lonely, dark nights
You are an angel sent from above
To fulfil the mission of everyone's wish

Sharing your wisdom lighting me up
Offering your hands and cheering me up
Energy of hope you show me in
Leading on to pathway that is lit up and never ends

You touch the heart of many souls
Giving hope and courage to be strong
Spread the lights you carry on
To make the world a better place to live.

Jalan Jalan Photography & Poetry

Gemma Escolano

ARTIST STATEMENT

IHSAN

ABOUT THE POEM:

One early morning on the train heading to my work, it was early March 2018. I'm browsing my social media page, suddenly my eyes caught on this page saying, "psychic". Out of curiosity, I open this, and I met the fellow who became my adviser, mentor and best friend. That's what this poem all about.

ABOUT THE IMAGE:

A guy from Lahor, Pakistan. He is young entrepreneur, running his own business. His dream is to visit other countries before he settles down. A guy who is kind-hearted and always ready to help others, helping is his inspiration.

"A MILLION YEARS OF TIME"

By: Gemma Escolano

I see you from bouquet of yellow daffodils lovely flowers
The smell and fragrance awaken my senses
The colour of your lips, like blood in my veins
The softness of your face, touch, like, cotton from my pillow
The sweetness of your smile, melting my lonely heart

Your eyes, like, brilliant stars from above
Shining full of life, full of happiness
Lighting up, in the middle of darkness
Guiding me, where my path is heading

I hear you, from the soft music of songs
Every lyric of love that swinging on me
Every tune, of sweet lovely melody
A lullaby, touches my heart, deep inside me

Humming birds, cross my path way
Saying your name, singing to me
You are the winds, beneath my wings
Flying with me over the lake of happiness

I feel you, every morning of sunrise
Smiling at me, with your bright lovely face
Covering me, with your warm, comfort blanket
Until the sunset, hiding behind the quiet sea

Been waiting for you, a million years of time
Since a thousand days, I see the giant lights
Since a hundred nights, I walked in the darkness of nights
Since a day, when my heart beats, capturing the time.

ARTIST STATEMENT

A MILLION YEARS OF TIME

ABOUT THE POEM:

This poem is a cry of a soul longing for her loved one long time ago. This is like a mystery of love that whoever we meet, we always assume this is right one that we are waiting for, and then afterwards we regret and are disappointed from our expectation that it was not turning out right. Nothing to do but just keep going and wait, for the right time will come.

ABOUT THE IMAGE:

Taken at the river of Rosetta, Tasmania, Australia. Every morning of our one week stay, I grabbed myself to catch the early morning shine on this river of peace and quiet place.

"OPEN YOUR EYES"

by: Gemma Escolano

Open your eyes out to reality
The most you loved, doesn't exist
Only fantasy, the feelings you get
From the wrong person, who took your heart away

Millennium world, full of chaos and mysteries
You never know, whom you are talking to
Be vigilant, and be smart choosing
So you do not get dragged into the net of their choice

They tell you, all the sweetest, flowering words
The romantic way that you can't resist
Like, a music of soft lullaby, coming to your ears
That electrifies you, with fullness of love and happiness

Their venom, is so deadly and fatal
They kill you slowly, until the last drop of blood
They are heartless, with face of a monster
Like, a roaring lion, waiting to eat their favourite supper

They dig your emotional weaknesses
For you following what they wanted from you
Until you realised, you are in the ocean of blindness
About to drain, about to drown, you can't breathe at all

They steal, not only your soft loving heart
But your dreams, your hopes and your future to come
But they leave you empty handed with wounded heart
The nightmare of your life, leave a mark in your heart

They wore a white mask, hiding their real colours
Using famous identities, for you to believe
Seems they are an angels, but with the wings of monsters
Pointed horn, ready to stab your innocent heart

Open your eyes, and see the real world
Not all the brilliant diamond are real
Not all the shining stones are genuine
Not all the beautiful faces are Princes
The best thing to do is open your eyes.

Jalan Jalan Photography & Poetry
Gemma Escolano

ARTIST STATEMENT

OPEN YOUR EYES

ABOUT THE POEM:

Awareness is the best tool to protect yourself from fallacious kind of people, the bad motives that deeply affect those victimised by this sort of scam. This is the inspiration that came to me when I wrote this poem.

ABOUT THE IMAGE:

I came home from work that afternoon. It was around 7 O'clock, already night time but the Sun still up. When Summer time here in Australia, the hours of day are longer compared to Winter time. The Sun is still up and sets mostly around 9pm. At that moment, when the Sun started going down, the colours of skies and the clouds was magnificent. Mixing with orange and yellow was superb and vivid. I love this combination of colours, lively and radiant. I'm in hurry to get my camera to take this fabulous sunset knowing that the Sun was quickly hiding down from far away. I love that moment, the energy around gives happiness and peace. The beautiful sunset from Western, Suburb, NSW, Australia.

"MY OWN LITTLE WAY"

By: Gemma Escolano

Let me love you, in my own little way
Let me give you, my thought and caring way
Let me hug you, my warmth embracing way
Let me dream of you, in my time in a different way

You know, that I love you, always calls to mind
I felt this, growing inside, each in everyday
I felt you, in my heart, with no reason to say
I felt you, within me, with no question to ask

Love is a magic, the old folk say
Unpredictable feelings, that knock your heart away
No objective form to touch, but you feel the softness
No fragrance to smell, but you own the blossoms

Love, is like, a butterfly, roaming inside you
Feeling light, feeling warm, electrifies within you
Vivid wings, floating around, in all the angles of your eyes
A magnificent paradise, only seen by your naked eyes

Love is all that matters, that's what we believe
No matter how apart our ages
No matter how reverent our beliefs
No matter how far our inter-space will be
Love is all that matters, all that matters is love.

ARTIST STATEMENT

MY OWN LITTLE WAY

ABOUT THE POEM:

The feelings of love and what is love?; can be read in this poem. We can share and we can give love to everyone in our different way, even in small things love is always there. Appreciate those little things from our loved ones. The time is not the same every day. We treasure the moment and we treasure the love.

ABOUT THE IMAGE:

The clouds that covered the mountain from far away caught my attention to shoot this image. It was a beautiful morning in the place where we stay at Rosetta, Tasmania. The colours of the trees and leaves, the reflection of the Sun and the clouds on the mountain, the perfect moment to feel the wonder of Nature.

"A CANDLE OF YOU"

By: Gemma Escolano

The silent night, creeping on me
Like, echoing, from the high mountain
Lost, in the middle of the road
Leading nowhere, heading somewhere

Thinking and thoughts, empty, like balloon
Going to the air with no direction
Heart saying, "Follow your lovely heart"
Brain saying, "Use your brilliant mind"

Many things to learn, like a child learning the first step
Many things to think, absorbing good knowledge
Many experiences to have, for us to be incredibly strong
Many down falls we had, for us to be absolutely tough

Many are calling, only a few that listened
Many have been told, but only a small of number followed
Staying blind to what matters most
Being deaf to what the very best

About time to light the candle, the power within us
The power to make, our own path of destiny
The power to create, our own sources of wealth
The power to cultivate, the dream of happiness of life
The power to give, the endless love to each and everyone

Life is continuous race, no one knows the end
Life keeps on going, though you meet the bend
Life is marvellous, if you find the right path for you
Life is wonderful if you get the right choice for you.

Jalan Jalan Photography & Poetry
Gemma Escolano

ARTIST STATEMENT

A CANDLE OF YOU

ABOUT THE POEM:

This poem is about life. Majority of people don't know what their purpose in life, their mission and what they have to contribute and share with others and to the world itself. Some people know their mission by knowing themselves. This will be the light to give to others to help them to find the right path for them. The title represents the light of candle that every one of us has, an inner lights that needs to ignite and be light to others.

ABOUT THE IMAGE:

I took this photo inside my bedroom, a scented candle in a crystal glass, underneath is a mirror tray. I added three carnation flowers to compensate the candle.

'THE BRIGHTER SIDE OF LIGHT"

By: Gemma Escolano

Look upon the dark cloudy day
You can see the bright light of Sun
Look upon the darkest night
You can see the brightly shining stars

Even if you are in the middle of turmoil situation
That you think it's never ending
Even if you are in the deep toxic relationship
That you think you can't escape the reality

Even if you are in the box of pain and sorrow
That you think that you can't find the way out
Even you are in the cage of misery and agony
That you think, life is throwing upon you

There's always tomorrow that shines for you
Giving you courage and perseverance
There's always hope that you can embrace
Giving you strength and happiness

There's always light to reach your dream
That all you love to do, it is one touch away
There's always a helping hand to lift you up
Showing you, life is wonderful and beautiful

Believe in yourself, that you have a power within you
Believe the process that everything will come in time
Believe that the present moment will not take so long
Believe in miracle that everything will align for you.

ARTIST STATEMENT

THE BRIGHTER SIDE OF LIGHT

ABOUT THE POEM:

I Remember one of my friends who posted in her face book page the words of depression from her life situation, the struggling that she has, is like there's no hope for her. Her story gave me inspiration to write this poem.

ABOUT THE IMAGE:

The morning sunrise slowly showing up from behind the mountain at the river of Tasmania. The frozen breeze of a morning day, the calm of river flowing matching with the singing bird. A magnificent morning from the land of Tasmania, Australia. I took hundreds of photos to have the best image.

"SAVE YOUR LOVE FOR ME"

By: Gemma Escolano

You left me, with a broken heart
Shattered into pieces, hard to pick them up
So much pain, can't bear for long
Dying inside, I don't know how to get up

Tear drops flowing from my eyes
Sobbing constantly, that I can't hold on to
Like, a fountain that flows, and has nowhere to go
Never know, where the end heading to

Those precious times, we spent together
I thought, the time would last forever
Those happy things, that we shared each other
I never knew it would end forever

How can I stand by myself?
Without you, comforting me, by my side
Without your helping hand, when I needed your pieces of advice
Without your caring heart, when I'm feeling down

But the time, quickly passes by for me
After a few decades, I totally healed
Moving on, my own life, without you
Embracing a new chapter in my life

Then now, out of the blue
You popping up without any clue
Trying to recall, the footprint left behind
Pressing the memories so that nothing is hiding

I don't know, what to say
It's like only, yesterday
Only the words I heard
"Save your love for me"

Jalan Jalan Photography & Poetry
Gemma Escolano

ARTIST STATEMENT

SAVE YOUR LOVE FOR ME

ABOUT THE POEM:

This poem is about love story of a girl who is madly in love with this guy but he left her without any promises. How can she cope with the feelings of loneliness and emptiness.? How can she manage to move on after that heartbroken moment.? Then, after decades for some reason they met each other and the guy is trying to get back the love that he left behind. This inspiration came to me from the person who is very close to my heart.

ABOUT THE IMAGE:

It was a lovely afternoon and the Sun slowly hiding from the mountain. The reflection of the sun rays illuminate the river water with crystal shine. A quite place in the middle of Wiseman Ferry, NSW Australia. Closer to the water, mountain and wild life. A lovely place to relax and have a family picnic.

"WHEN THE TIME COMES"

By: Gemma Escolano

Don't look at my lovely face
It will fade when the time comes
Don't look at my long brown colour hair
It will turn into grey hair
When I reach my golden years

Don't look at my dark brown magnetic eyes,
It will turn into double vision
When my life begins at forty
Don't look at my silky and fair skin,
They will wrinkle, when the time comes

Don't look at my kissable red lips
They will crumple, like smash paper
When I forget to apply my favourite lipsticks
Coz Alzheimer's almost swallows my memories

Don't look upon my long legged legs
They are full of varicose veins due to my long standing work
Don't look at my attractive and perfect body
It will become saggy and dull due to unhealthy diet

Look upon the love that I save for you
It will mesmerise and last forever
Look upon the way I care,
It will give you comfort and warmth feeling

Look upon my deep affection
It gives you security and contentment
Look upon the light that I share with you
It will show you the brighter path for you

Look upon the time I spend with you
It is priceless and meaningful
It is colourful and wonderful
Look upon me, and feel the love that I have given.

Jalan Jalan Photography & Poetry
Gemma Escolano

ARTIST STATEMENT

WHEN THE TIME COMES

ABOUT THE POEM:

The inspiration came to me about the human age especially women. How they look like when they still young, then after a few decades it will change slowly, until they realise they are not young anymore. Everything changed, everything erodes as time goes by. There's no things that stay permanent, no one remain young, so they need to embrace the reality of life. The beautiful and stunning physical appearance were vanished by time, but the real beauty comes from the heart. The personality, attitude and most importantly genuine love, are what makes the whole and the essence of a women.

ABOUT THE IMAGE:

It was warm and beautiful afternoon, me and my mum wanting to catch that moment. I grab my camera and start taking photos in front of our place. Pretending we are in the park, that no one can disturb our craziness time. The high light of this moment was our bonding, laughing and giggling together even the smallest things that makes us happy, freeing our mind from the real world and being happy whatever it will be.

"NOSTALGIC LOVE"

By: Gemma Escolano

The wave feelings of mine, came from ancient culture
Reminiscences from the deep mine of gold
Ocean of memories came back to me
The rapid feelings of happiness in me

Full of softness and tenderness
Full of magnificent love and sweetness
Clouds of paradise that never end
Embracing the moment to reach the end

The glimpse in the happiness of love
Feeling from deep inside, a nostalgic love
Part of the clothing wrapped around my heart
Comforting and securing, keeping warmth in my heart

Rainbow colours, seen everywhere
Vivid to see, never touch, but felt everywhere
Synchronised and connected from the past
Just feel it today, digest and don't make it fast

Highest feelings of vibration, no other than love
A magical feeling, that brought the memories of love
Catching the moment in the happiness for love
Nothing to deny, nothing to hide, these feelings of love.

Jalan Jalan Photography & Poetry
Gemma Escolano

ARTIST STATEMENT

NOSTALGIC LOVE

ABOUT THE POEM:

This nostalgic love poem, inspired me about how is the feelings of emotion of being loved and be loved?. If you are in the mid of these kind of feelings, everything was full of wonderful and happiness. The highest point of vibration of the heart is when the people are happy about being in love. The nostalgic experience can heal and transform the feelings of stress, weakness and pain, physically, emotionally and spiritually into the productive mind. Happy thoughts and the synergy that works for the best result.

ABOUT THE IMAGE:

This photo was a day before my mum's birthday (15 May 2019). We flew to Tasmania for a week to spend for her birthday celebration, as well as to do my project. The background is the Richmond Bridge located in the North of Hobart Tasmania, Australia. This is the oldest stone bridge that is listed as heritage in history of Australia. Built 1823 up to 1825 by the hands of convict labourers, who gave their effort to build this bridge which is an honour to them having benefited generations of people. The stunning and breathtakingly beautiful scenery around the area is magnificent.

"FALLACIOUS LOVE"

By: Gemma Escolano

Your appearance, came unexpectedly
From unknown place in different time zone
Surprised me, with your friendly gesture
Simple "Hi", your starting point to say
Conversation begin with your eagerness

Time that passed by so quickly
I found myself, closer to your side
I got easily drawn, with your magnetic appeal
From your sugar coated fantasy words
Making me believe and feel I'm above the clouds

Your sweetness, and loving thought
The love affection that seems so real
Easily caught, any woman that can win the hearts
Without any single time thinking
On what this is all about?

Until the moment, goes upside down
The wind changes to other direction
Gets lost, in the middle of nowhere
Blind, into enchanted wilderness
Hard to find myself, back into reality

Where is, the love that you offered me?
Where is, the dream that you shared with me?
Where is the future that you planned to create for me?
Where are, the promises that you gave to me?
Where is, the man that I loved so dear?

My mind, blowing away
And bursting, into constant tears
When I found out, that your love was untrue
When I realised, you are a big, fat, ugly, giant wolf
Eating me alive, to get what you want

There's no space on Earth for a person like you
You are like a tamed snake, but has deadly venom
Your heart was cold, like, glacier from Alaska
Your face, like an angel, but has a red eyes at night
Dungeon in the lake of fires, the better place suited for you.

Jalan Jalan Photography & Poetry
Gemma Escolano

ARTIST STATEMENT

FALLACIOUS LOVE

ABOUT THE POEM:

This poem is about the story of romance. At first, it seems real, but at the end the truth will reveal the real motives and the interest of this man. He has shown his love from the start, but it turns into fallacious love. The intense feeling of love turned into grudge and hatred from this experience.

ABOUT THE IMAGE:

The stairs on the top of the mountain of Mount Willington, the highest mountain in Hobart, Tasmania, Australia. The view is breathtaking from the top and you can see the whole place of Hobart. Don't miss out going up on the top of this mountain when you visit Tasmania, it's worth your time to see and experience the beauty of Nature. I love every corner of Tasmania.

"ETERNAL BLAZE"

By: Gemma Escolano

One soul, since the time of Creation
Fire of blanket, formed, split and landed in two bodies
Originated from above, sent by the hand of Master
Mission reborn, fulfilling the mysteries of life

Walking on earth, separated, in place and time
Blocking the memories, innate, since from the past
Flying thoughts, of never ending vastness
Searching for the answer of who you really are?

Life mysteries, continuous day after day
With no path direction, where you heading, everyday
Finding yourself, is your main aspiration
Dreaming of something wonderful, is your inspiration

For many centuries, you visited the Earth
Amazed with the wonderful life, that Creator has given you
And yet, something missing, deep within you
Still longing, looking around you for answer

Many significant things happened in your life
Giving you the clue, that Universe is always watching you
Grabbing the moment, thinking for yourself
That, the only answer, was sitting in your core higher self

Until one day, your life changes drastically
Your eyes are open wide to reality
Awakening your soul is the first thing to know
To understand the myth, of the whole mysteries of life

Come to understand, someone same as you, was searching too
For the concept and thought like fantasising the implausible
That Settling for a relationship, that feels merely comfortable
It is possible to form an even deeper magnetic connection,
Coz, you are the twin flames, magnificent, created as one.

Jalan Jalan Photography & Poetry
Gemma Escolano

ARTIST STATEMENT

ETERNAL BLAZE

ABOUT THE POEM:

This is all about the Twin Flames, how they were created a long time ago. This is related to the word they called "Soul Mate", but twin flames has deeper meaning compared to soulmate. Everything in this poem tells the story of what is the meaning of Twin Flames.

ABOUT THE IMAGE:

It was a warm and lovely day in the middle Summer. I was in hurry to press my shutter on my camera to catch the sunset. Everything in this photo was synchronised to each other, the colours, time and weather, reason this turning up unexplainable and magical beauty given by Nature.

"DON'T EVER LEAVE ME"

by: Gemma Escolano

"Don't ever leave me" the words, whispering to me
Two different occasions, you remind me of this
Seems, there's feeling inside you, the fear of losing me
Coming up to surface, of your blowing thought and worries

How strong, is your love for me?
How far, your feeling, towards me?
How faithful, is your love for me?
How is the trust, you are giving me?

Is this because, we are far apart?
Between the distance, miles away
Between the time, night and day
Just because, we haven't seen yet in any way

Physically apart, but one in heart
Different minds, but one in thought
Different beliefs, but one in soul
Different vortexes, but one in energy

The love that we're connected by is like;
A giant, deep ocean where no one knows the end
Above the waves and clouds, sky is the limit
A Universe of galaxies, the vastness of million, shining stars

Set aside, your worries and fears
Faith in your heart, no matter what
We live this life, searching to one another
Until we find, our divine path, destiny together.

Jalan Jalan Photography & Poetry
Gemma Escolano

ARTIST STATEMENT

DON'T EVER LEAVE

ABOUT THE POEM:

This love poem tells the feelings of fear and worries, how sometimes the thought feed our subconscious mind and manifests it onto surface of reality. Mind is so strong to think many things, it can break our heart or make it, depends on how we accept and choose what we want to feed in our mind. Love and hope are the strongest feelings to defend and to conquer the fear in our mind as well as our heart.

ABOUT THE IMAGE:

Image shot is the beautiful view of Watson Bay, Sydney, Australia from a place called the Federation cliff walk. You can see the amazing panoramic views of the Pacific Ocean. The silent deep blue colour of the sea gives harmony to this breathtaking scene. These sandstone cliffs around this area are the sentry that protects the whole City of Sydney. Walking around this place on a nice day and a smooth breeze was amazing. You can see the greenery bottle brushes flowering and some exotic plants. Added to this are the singing birds flying around.

"LINKING CONNECTION"

by: Gemma Escolano

The forces of unseen, but known to people
Fed by thought and strong desires, will of human
Entirely govern, the life of a living one
Walking on Earth a life journey began

Hidden treasures, unknown to many
Of this power created from above
Only few people, have their eyes open to see
Using these, as sword of their brilliant success

Power beneath, since birth of Creation
Birth right being to use endless potential of wealth
Bring into reality, as you commanded to see
Strong connectivity that no human had foreseen

Planted the seed, of healthy and productive mind
Feeds with happy thoughts, desiring and faith
Cultivates the knowledge, of abundant mind of creation
Digging the feelings, intense quavers of emotion

The will of human, freed and given by Almighty
Only for people, what is their path being taken?
Make the best choice, and be your guiding star
Ignite the linking connection, sleeping deep within you

Grasp this Infinite reality, embrace and never let it go
The sources of life, guiding you to the best of you
Never denying, never hiding, this linking connection
The portal sources, the powerful link to Infinite Intelligence.

Jalan Jalan Photography & Poetry
LITO C UYAN

ARTIST STATEMENT

LINKING CONNECTION

ABOUT THE POEM:

I love the deepness of this poem, after I wrote this, I was amazed at the outcome. The poem about our inner self, higher self, instinct or the gut feeling. The small voice that is guiding us about the things that we need to consider. This voice inside us is our higher self that is connected to our main source of life. Try to have your moment, free your mind from outer world, suddenly you can experience the feelings of fulfilment and happiness when you find your higher self.

ABOUT THE IMAGE:

The person who took this image is Mr. Lito C. Uyan, one of the contributing photographers of Corbis NY and formerly one of Art Directors of ABS-CBN Corporation, Philippines. The image tells the story of voyage ship waiting for passengers to board and sail to far away foreign land. The beautiful purple light around the area from the reflection of sunset has given this image fullness of life. The magnificent horizon was perfectly timed when taking this image. A very good place to have a stroll with friends or loved ones and watching the sunset in this beautiful place of Manila Bay, Manila Philippines.

"I SET YOU FREE"

By: Gemma Escolano

I don't know what to say, after the words I heard?
Everything is falling apart, from unexpected words
Feeling numb, my whole body, my soul, from reality
The Earth suddenly stops, revolving for me

You hurting me so much, deeply through my heart
You made me cry, as my days turned into grey of sadness
You made me crazy, to accept and love you
But you are dropping me, from your fabrications and pretensions

Lies and untruth was the love you gave and offered me
Pretending, all false of beauties and sweetness
All wonderful dreams turned into ashes
Of pain and bitterness scattered on the ground

My thinking, you are my long and lasting love
My understanding, you are my partner for better and for worse
My perception, you are my knight with a shining armour
My anticipation, you are my half beloved heart, in your victory

And now, you are begging me to forgive you
For what you have done to me
For all the lies that you are telling me
For your pathological false promises

I think there's no room yet for now
Coz, I gave you all, my whole hearted love and affection
I think, there's no time yet for now
Cause, I shared with you, my hopes, my dreams, and my visions

All I can say is, "Thank you for everything"
You gave me, the best remarkable lesson
That, "don't trust and don't give your heart easily to someone"
Now, I setting you free, coz, you are not totally deserving
To have and keep my pure, caring and loving heart.

Jalan Jalan Photography & Poetry
Gemma Escolano

ARTIST STATEMENT

I SET YOU FREE

ABOUT THE POEM:

This is all about the after breakup moment of two lovers. The feeling of pain and sadness after the breakup. She gave all the love, affection, attention and time all of her life, but unfortunately they end up separating. The guy was trying to gain the forgiveness for what he has done. Accepting that they are not meant to be is the way to let go the heartache, pain and sadness from all the expectation within the relationship. Accepting and forgiveness for pain is the best and only way to let go and set you free.

ABOUT THE IMAGE:

Taken in Hobart, Tasmania, Australia, the river from the suburb of Rosetta. That was dawn, with the Sun starting to show. The tranquillity of peace I felt in this place was so amazing with the catch of the morning breeze and the Sun behind the mountain was superb. No one can beat the beauty given by Nature.

"THE SHADOW OF YOUR SOUL"

by: Gemma Escolano

I can see you, but I can't touch you
I can feel you, but I can't hug you
I'm whispering to you,
but you can't hear me
I'm looking at you,
but you can't see through me

Here I am, always watching you
Like, a movie on the wide screen
Every move of your body,
every twinkling of your eyes
Every smile, every laugh,
every sad face, of you

You are the Moon, seen far away
Your bright shining light, rejuvenates my spirit
Even you are hiding, from the clouds all night
I'm still seeing you from behind

You can't get away from me
I'm always hiding in your mind
Even if you're not thinking of me
But you feel my loving spirit inside you

I am with you, all the time
Even if you're not recognising me
Even if you're not noticing me
But you know, beneath, within you, I'm always around

If you felt you are losing me, the mirror is the answer
Look upon yourself, you can see me deep-seated in your eyes
You can feel me, rooted in your longing soul
Just close your eyes, you can catch a glimpse of me, clear and bright.

Jalan Jalan Photography & Poetry
LITO C UYAN

ARTIST STATEMENT

THE SHADOW OF YOUR SOUL

ABOUT THE POEM:

This poem is all about the soul within our body. This is our infinite part of being, who we are inside and outside. The explanation in this poem of how the unseen plane of our self, the higher version of us, wants to communicate and to remind us of our existence. In this case, the shadow in the poem keep reminding the person to recognise the existence of life deeper within our body.

ABOUT THE IMAGE:

This image is perfect for this poem, signifying the shadow of the soul. Inside the prison cell is the statue of Dr. Jose Rizal, the National Hero of the Philippines. After Spanish colonised the Philippines for more than Three Hundred years, Dr. Jose Rizal came and gave inspiration to his fellow Filipinos through his intellect, brilliance and creative writing, done with love and sincerity for his country's people. Through his writing, he awoke the heart and mind of most Filipino people to the corruption and fault of the Spanish government. Aside from being known as a Medical Doctor, has also possessed lots of talents as a poet, an essayist, a painter, a sketch artist, and a sculptor. Spanish rule in the Philippines ended in the year 1898, but to this day, the shadow of his soul still remains in the heart of Filipinos. This image from Fort Santiago, Manila, Philippines was shot by Lito C. Uyan, one of the best Photographers from the Philippines.

"PLEASE TRY TO FORGIVE ME"

by: Gemma Escolano

You just easily say, these words to me
After you broke my heart, into tormented pieces of me
After you left me, in the middle of the dark and sadness
After you vanished, in pain and in agony

My mind blowing away, I don't know what to think?
My body was shivering, from the pain inside
My heart beating faster, racing in a field of strain
Every word you are throwing at me stabbing into my heart

Why is this happening to us?
What's wrong with us?
Why have you changed your mind?
What is the matter with you?

We're just starting, to build our bridge to paradise
Reaching out for us to get to our goals and visions
We're just starting, to tighten our rope of happiness
For us, holding hand together, facing our promising future

And then everything turns into countless bubbles
Popping away, into the air of unknown reality
Every promise, erased in a split second of moment
Every wave of dreams, flashing away, into the rock of shock

How can I smile at the sunrise, without your morning note?
How can I enjoy my noon time, without you, checking on me?
How can I relieve my tired days, without your warm and comforting words?
How can I have my sound sleep, without you, saying goodnight?

Many hours you begging me to forgive you
Maybe, when it is time, I can't feel the pain anymore?
Might be at the stage when I am totally healed from your heartless mind?
Could be, one day when I totally forget, all about you?

ARTIST STATEMENT

PLEASE TRY TO FORGIVE ME

ABOUT THE POEM:

This poem was the feelings after they broke up, the love after being together for quite long years. This is the saddest part of two lovers in a relationship, how both of them never think this could be happen. The intense feelings of how she copes with everyday life after the life she has been used to. Like a shocking event where everything changed drastically and was turned upside down.

ABOUT THE IMAGE:

Image taken during my short visit in Philippines. The beach from Barrio Pulang Daga, Negros Occidental, Philippines. About eight (8) hour drive, catch by bus from Pasay Terminal in Manila going to the province of Daet. The quiet and shady afternoon, the soothing breeze, the warm sands, the sounds of waves, the swaying leaves of coconut trees, all together connected to each other. This place is inviting to relaxation and sitting by the beach, just to feel the serenity of Nature. The best place away from the noise of City life.

"ALL I NEED"

by: Gemma Escolano

All I need is nothing more, than your sweetest smile
Killing my soul, with your enigmatic rays of sunshine
Your magical, kissable lips, touching me so amply
Travel into my core, within myself, so your mine

All I need is nothing more, than the warmth of your tender hug
Squeezing my spirit into my highest longing
Swaying every dance, with the beat of rhythm soul
Flying into the air, the feelings of love that never

All I need is nothing more, than your twinkling eyes
Looking deep into the abyss, of my wondering mind
Melting my innermost, melancholic heart of mine
Telling me, with speechless words, that you are mine

All I need is nothing more, than you're soft and tender touch
Roving along, into the river, of my awakening soul
A long and winding voyage, of endless gentle love
Showing me, that you are always mine

All I need is nothing more, than your eloquent presence
Facing life's mysteries, happening day by day
Rain and shine, you always with me, side by side
Giving strength and moulding me into the best of me

All I need is nothing more, than your faithful heart
Loving me unconditionally, without asking for more
Caring for me with endless time, without feeling sore
Locking me up with your promises,
That your Heart will always be mine alone.

ARTIST STATEMENT

ALL I NEED

ABOUT THE POEM:

This poem is all about the feeling of love. The longing of heart to feel the true love that she's waiting for for a long time. The deep feelings, the sincerity without any demand or expectation, is to only love her unconditionally and faithfully from the core of heart.

ABOUT THE IMAGE:

This place taken in Richmond the suburb of Hobart, Tasmania, NSW Australia. The large grass where I am seating is near the Richmond Bridge, famous for being the oldest bridge in Australia. It was a quiet afternoon and the weather was good for going around.

"DARLING ALEENA"

by: Gemma Escolano

"So many nights, I'm dreaming of you
So many days, I'm waiting for you
Looking for an answer....but yet, no response
Like a tape recorder in my mind....Where are you?"

The little girl, seating behind the door
Hiding from pain, but no one cares, no one knows
The pain in longing for someone dear, closer to her heart
The love that she never had, since the day she saw the light

Pale and skinny Darling Aleena, deprived of everything
Exiguity of material things to make her happy
Lack of something that she needed the most
And the worst part, hunger for love that she never felt

Raised up in different families, one after another
It seemed so confusing, it seemed so complicated
But she can't complain, and needed to embrace the existence
Accepted and let go, the flow of life in mystical way

Tears of sadness and loneliness flowed from her eyes
Hiding from others, hiding from reality
"Why am I different from other girls like me?
Why is my life not normal, like other child could be?"

"A child full of happiness, full of love
A daughter full of care, from the love of parents
A kid full of laughter, full of joy and dreams
A young girl, an adorable and beautiful, little Princess"

"Here I am, a dagger in my hand, thinking to end this agony
Something to forget, the hurt rooted within me
Something to end, the life that I never dreamt of
But...suddenly...I stopped, popping into my mind"

"No...this is not right, I don't want to hurt myself this way
I want to be happy, like other kids, full of life that meant to be
I want to feel, I am precious, lovable and winsome daughter
I want to be cared for, to be cherished, and to be wanted"

Darling Aleena, don't be sad, don't cry
Step out behind the door of despair and emptiness
Your brilliant future and remarkable happiness,
Waiting and waving at you, to claim and prosper
You are magnificent, delightful and sweet Darling Aleena.

ARTIST STATEMENT

DARLING ALEENA

ABOUT THE POEM:

It was long time ago, I remember this child who suffered from loneliness and sadness from being away from her parent. Left by her mother in care of other families one after another was the last option for them to survive in order to work for a living. In her early age, she managed to cope with what life is throwing at her, even though many questions on her mind of what life she has and what is to come? This is a vibrant of memory, it's like only yesterday.

ABOUT THE IMAGE:

I took this photo at my place. The stuffed toy of teddy bear represents the girl, Darling Aleena, who was always hiding and throwing herself behind the door. Every time she was lonely, upset and disappointed, behind the door was her comfort zone. This photo taken late afternoon when the rays of the Sun passing through the door reflect the light on to the stuffed toy.

"THE BATTLE WITHIN"

By: Gemma Escolano

What life goes on?...What lies get on?
Self of unknown, walking around blindfolded
Like an Autumn leaf, blown where the wind takes you
Swept and dumped, where the gutter catches you

Went with the run, of the crazy, rocky, river flow
Without thinking of, what is beyond this endless row?
Without any plan, of what is the best path to take?
Yet, finger pointing at others, when the storm intake

So many wants in life, so many dreams in mind
And yet, nothing to commit to, just only whispering
And you letting go of the lucky days coming for you
Without holding the moment changing everything

Life goes on and on with you, always waiting and hoping
And yet you always freeze with fear and anxiety
You never tried, to do new things, to start ahead
Hopeless and helpless, are the only things in your head

So many questions arise, filing up for more
But you always stuck from the intense pain of your past
Embedded with regrets and endless frustration
Like a shadow of the ghost, always following you around

You have to start, to find your inner self
Let go of the past, that can't help you to strive
Release the hatred, pasted in your inner core
Empty your heart of deep grudges and long bitterness

There's always a helping hand, when you seek, and pursue it
There's always ears for you, to listen to your never ending stories
There's always a comforting hand, to hug and accept your imperfections
There's always a genuine heart to love you more than your expectation

Look upon, and follow the lights to your brighter tomorrow
Open your mind, to see the opportunities, that you we're looking for
Listen to the magical voice, a message, comes from infinite higher self
Live with your heart open, and embrace the love, that Universe has given you.

Jalan Jalan Photography & Poetry
Gemma Escolano

ARTIST STATEMENT

THE BATTLE WITHIN

ABOUT THE POEM:

When I wrote this poem, the thought that came to me was all about life. Majority of people dreaming of something wonderful, but few are daring to do to make it happen. Due to upsets through their life journey, they freeze in those circumstances and hurdles, the reason most of dreams will be set aside.

ABOUT THE IMAGE:

The image was in Sydney, Australia. I was in the ferry when I took this photo of Opera House, (the icon of Australia) with the boat in front of me. It was a cloudy afternoon and about to rain, but it was a beautiful day to go around in this beautiful City of Sydney.

"LET IT BE AND LET IT GO"

by: Gemma Escolano

Life must go on, a never ending journey
Like a river flowing into the wilderness of truth
Winding water running down the path,
Thoughts flowing away from,
Shallow into deeper, quieter water

Along the way, smooth and rough
Moments, touching your heart
As you go by, growing into adult of mystical race
Life getting intense with experiences faced everyday
Mind and thought always confused,
About what's this by the way?

Trying to survive what life is throwing at you
Accepting the reality, thinking this is life meant to be
But, the vast of majority of people, we're blind to the streams of growth
Never knowing the mission behind the reason why we are alive

Collective mind that absorbs, since the day you we're born
Conditioning mind, feed and rooted from undeniable environment
The patterns that block the fullest expression of yourself
Hiding behind, the shadow of your lonely, hunger soul

Let go of the burden in your heart that is weighing you down
Let it throw out all the clutters in your heart, that block your potential to grow
Let's forget the bad memories that happened in the past
Let the scars of yesterday be forgotten, and buried in the crevasses of memories

Start knowing yourself for who you really are
Finding your inner-self, the starting point of your happiness
Discovering your seat of awareness, and presence of consciousness
And living your life, from the depth of your magnificent and beautiful being

Let it open your heart to the wonderful life that is designed to be
Let it flow with the vivid radiance of light, embedded in your longing spirit
Let your energy fly away, into the highest frequency of yourself
And spread the love to each and every one, for this is the mission of all humanity.

Jalan Jalan Photography & Poetry
Gemma Escolano

ARTIST STATEMENT

LET IT BE AND LET IT GO

ABOUT THE POEM:

The inspiration that came to me when I wrote this poem is about the journey of our life. No exception, all people can experience different norms in life, unexpected events that occur since we start growing up. We must be aware of things around us and in the case of upsets we need to learn how to let go all unnecessary things that never deserving us or helping us. Learning from it and moving on with a positive mind is the best that we can do.

ABOUT THE IMAGE:

I was standing on the jetty, river of Rosetta in Hobart, Tasmania, Australia. The Sun ray's reflection goes to my face. I felt in that moment the peacefulness and serenity of that morning. It's like I am flying like a bird, closer to Nature, closer to my heart. Feeling of happiness from inside will manifest in outside world.

"THE LADY OF FAITH AND COURAGE"

By: Gemma Escolano

Walking along in the dark lonely night
You don't know where you heading to?
You don't know who, you ask for help?
Holding in your arms the sweet little angel
Innocent of what is going on

No one accepting you and what your life was dealing you
No one understand you, that you needed a little help
No one helping you and offering some room to rest
No one beside you, only the little girl, always smiling at you
The only one, who gives you the reason to breathe

"What is happening to me?.. Why don't they understand me?
Why don't they accept me for what I am facing now?
Is this my fault?....to love someone, who is not ready to be the one?
Is it right not to be a perfect person accepted by this cruel society?"
Asking yourself all these questions over and over again

It was long ago but these memories hang around haunting you
You've been through a lot of hard time, you've been in a lot of awful situations
People despised you, even the least person you expected to stand with you
Everyone against of you, you are a loser, you are helpless
That's the way they think of you, that's the way they showed to you

But you fight silently, in spite the society not accepting you
You have nothing, only the little one that God entrusted to you
You need to survive, you need to be brave, you need to be strong
Bow your head, knee on the ground, praying and whispering
That is always in your mind, the faith in your heart, the courage in your soul

No one heard your crying, no one knows your pain
No one comforted you, no one listened to you
Struggling all the way to face the battle of your life
You stand straight and full of confidence to fight
Thinking the victory will be yours at the end

Now, looking back all those painful time of hardship
You win the chain of trials, you reach the ladder of success
But your feet are still on the ground with humility and forgiveness
Your big heart always open for those who are in need
Your faith, love and courage go beyond timeless and priceless.

Jalan Jalan Photography & Poetry
Gemma Escolano

ARTIST STATEMENT

THE LADY OF FAITH AND COURAGE

ABOUT THE POEM:

This poem is dedicated to the woman who is very close to my heart, who opened my eyes and led me to this wonderful Earth, to experience happy and sad moment. Who taught me how to be strong, independent, kind to others, with strong beliefs and determination to achieve the dreams of what I want to be. Her life experiences makes her stronger and able to conquer all the hindrances along her way. In spite all those bad experiences, she remains humble and has a big heart to help others.

ABOUT THE IMAGE:

The lady in this image is the strong woman I've ever known. I took this photo of her in the City of Hobart, Tasmania, Australia. Behind her are the line-up of boats resting and floating at the wharf. The last day of our stay in that place.

"MY SWEET SENSATION"

By: Gemma Escolano

Strange feelings came over me
Cannot express the commotion of fantasy
You brought me into this kind of ecstasy
Covering my whole senses within me

The sweet sensation that wraps around my body
No words to say, how intense these feelings are in me
Like the electric current, running and digging into my bone
I cannot control this sort of energy that is igniting my soul

There is something special about you
I can't figure out, the shape nor the taste
No script to comprehend, how been through this infatuation?
The only things I know, I have feelings for you

The mystical way of your endless sweet smile
Every time I look at you, a pretty glance of you
It's melting my heart away, like chocolate ice cream
Dripping from the cone, as a goblet for gladness

The sparkle glimpse of your look
Something hidden behind your twinkling eyes
I can't help myself, staring at you
Like a magnet, captivating and pulling me towards you

You make my day, every time I heard you're softly voice
I felt I'm flying above the clouds of wonders, love and beauty
Like a singing bird, singing and dancing the melody of joyfulness
That makes me fall into deep, sleep of happiness

Some vast array of connection between us
But I don't know where starting and how it begin
My wish is to give me some times of your precious moment
To acknowledge my feelings, my sweet sensation, the joy of my heart.

Jalan Jalan Photography & Poetry
Gemma Escolano

ARTIST STATEMENT

MY SWEET SENSATION

ABOUT THE POEM:

This poem is all about the intense feelings that can't be explained but are happening. The details of every words of how the expressive feelings of emotion are conveyed is in this poem. How important the person is being the subject of this poem.

ABOUT THE IMAGE:

The building across the river with purple lights was the Mona Museum located in Berriedale, Tasmania, Australia. This museum is combination of Old and New Art. From the city of Hobart you can catch a ferry going to this museum. Luckily I am with my mum and the place where we stayed was so close to this museum, only 20minutes walk away.

"YOU ARE THE ANSWER"

by: Gemma Escolano

Since the day, I felt you inside me
Hiding in the cocoon of magical creation
So much joy and happiness will be,
Every day that I am waiting for

As day passes by, as I am watching you
You form into magnificent, beautiful being
I heard every beat of your little heart
I felt every movement of your tiny body

Holding in my hand the rosary beads
Constantly, whispering and reciting everyday
That Almighty Creator would grant me
A delightful, graceful and lovely Princess

Few months over, you came into the light
I held you in my arms, so little adorable angel
Felicity and gladness, I had received
That God acknowledged, all my fervent prayers

You are a blessing from above, giving me joy and light
You fill my heart, expelling emptiness and sadness
You fulfil my dreams as being me, a mother with mission
To guide, care and love you, as I will be, coz, you are the answer

Now, you have grown up with beautiful soul and graceful lady
How thankful I am to have you and be a part of me
Your light and wisdom, add shine and glow on me
You are something wonderful that makes my heart beat peacefully.

ARTIST STATEMENT

YOU ARE THE ANSWER

ABOUT THE POEM:

This is about my one and only daughter. The story of my pregnancy with her. An expectant mother, the only wish and prayer is to have a baby girl. At that time, only a few expectant mothers go through ultra sounds due to expensive treatment and we can't afford to have one, better to wait and pray. By the grace of Almighty, my wish was granted. She was the answer to my prayer. The emotion of happiness can be read in this poem.

ABOUT THE IMAGE:

I took this photo at home from my bed. I used my daughter's picture when she was 4 years old. She was holding her two (2) favourite stuffed toys. Behind the picture was her lovely pink dress when she was 10 year old, the only dress I kept for her for long time. Now she is 20 year old, a sweet grown up young lady.

"THE PRECIOUS LIFE"

by: Gemma Escolano

The precious life we have, given by Almighty
Walking on Earth every single day
Stunning sunrise seen everyday
Waiting for sunset as circle of days

Every breeze we felt from nowhere
Touching our skin, so gentle and smooth
Every air we breathed, set as the fuel for life
Keeping us alive, for the beauty of life

Every person we met in every season of lives
Given us lessons, given us something to inspire
Sending from above, for us to see
The path that we we're meant to be on

Enjoy the life as we can, while we still young and strong
Seek your true mission, reason why we we're here on Earth
Find your true self, hiding within your soul
You will be found, the genuine and lasting happiness

Give your best in every step along the way
Cultivate and improve your unique gifted passion
Share the blessing that you possess
To gain more grace and to share more happiness

Give love to each in every soul you meet
By showing empathy and helping them to grow
Share the light that ignites within you
To open the way to their own path to take

The most precious of life, more than anything else
More than the pearl from the abyss of ocean
More than the gold from the depths of Earth
It is magnificent and sumptuous, glorifying the Creator.

ARTIST STATEMENT

THE PRECIOUS LIFE

ABOUT THE POEM:

This poem signifies the life that we need to treasure and give value. This inspiration came to me when I look at how our life is so precious, that every day we need to give the best in every angle of our lives and be mindful of everything around us. How we can contribute to improving our life as well as the life of people that are close to us.

ABOUT THE IMAGE:

This image taken in Richmond, Tasmania, Australia. The St. John's Catholic Church built in 1836, is considered the oldest church existing in Australia. One of the vibrant tourist spots in Richmond is the same place where the oldest bridge is located.

"FIGHT FOR LIFE"

by: Gemma Escolano

I want to ease these feelings inside
Want to let go and fly away from this internal pain
Missing you, I seriously realized
How hard it feels, when you're not around

Fight your own battle
It will be last very soon
God gave you another chance
For you to live and be alive

Hold and be strong
Keep fighting for your life
This is only for a while
And tomorrow you will be fine

I know it's hard for you
Laying down in your bed of life
Your mind is strong and sharp
But your weak body is trying to fight

You are prisoner of your stubborn mind
You always taking for granted what you already has
Now you realise, how precious is your life
You need to be aware and taking care of it

Your body was craving, for the quality of life
But you ignored it, with your denial attitude
Screaming louder in front of you
But you stayed deaf and continued what you want

And now, you cried out loud
Trying to get back what you missed out
But your body is deaf and keeps silent about what you want
And you trying to bring back, the energy and strength of your life.

101

ARTIST STATEMENT

FIGHT FOR LIFE

ABOUT THE POEM:

This poem is all about the person who is related to me. Six (6) months ago he had a stroke and stayed for three (3) months in the hospital. I wrote this at the time when he was in the emergency room after operation and sedated for three (3) days. Before the stroke happened, we're about to leave on that day going to Central Coast, NSW for a week holiday as well as to shoot my project. It was early Monday morning around 3 o'clock, at that moment I was sleeping, then suddenly I heard a big noise, hearing his voice asking for help but his speech was not clear. It was like his voice was like a drunk man, I only heard his loud voice. It was a big, surprising shock seeing him fallen down from the edge of the bed and not able to move half his body. I was panicked, but I did manage to ask the children to call the ambulance. I was devastated and completely shocked. From that day on everything was completely changed in our life's daily routine.

ABOUT THE IMAGE:

The image taken at our backyard home one morning. The rays of the Sun visibly touches in every corner of our backyard. A bright morning perfect for taking a very good photo. I use the Foot Stress Fracture Walking Boot as the subject of the image to represent the poetry. He used this Walking Boot when he start walking after three weeks of being bedridden, as part of his therapy to help his left foot back to normal walking.

"DARK SHADOW"

By: Gemma Escolano

I am in the dark shadow of the Moon
Wanting to escape, to see the face of a brilliant light
The first rays of the Moon every run of the time
Bathing in the moonlight, dancing with endless joy

I am in the dark shadow of a giant Sun
Wanting to step out ahead, to feel the warm comfort of
The first smile in the morning dawn
Every rise of this beautiful giant smile

I am in the dark shadow of a twinkling star
Wanting to touch the dust of a vivid shine
Twinkling of eyes with every pour of rainbow dust
Follow the fellows to light the dimness of the quiet night

I am in the dark shadow of this beautiful planet Earth
Wanting to merge, wanting to touch, to feel the life beyond
From greenery farm, walking and dancing with joy
From the abyss of sea, swimming and diving with endlessly
From the sky, flying and hiding in the sea of clouds

Here I am in the dark shadow, wanting to be free
From my hiding closet of silent emptiness
No one can hear, no one can see, no one knows that I am existing
Shout out loud, scream for long, cry for help
But no one cares...coz...they drawn away by their selfishness.

Jalan Jalan Photography & Poetry
Gemma Escolano

ARTIST STATEMENT

DARK SHADOW

ABOUT THE POEM:

I wrote this poetry referring to a soul who wants to step out of life that is full of trials, stress, hurdles, agony, sadness and loneliness. She wants to experience the life that she has not had before, to set her free from those mountains of miserable situations. She wants to fly and to see the beauty of life behind the curtain of darkness that surrounds her. She wants a key to unlock the chains that are holding her on the bed of hopelessness. She wants to recognise the beauty inside her heart. She wants to unleash the hidden talent that is wanting to explore and step out from the dark shadow that keeps dragging her into the abyss of despair. Sometimes, we need quietness to listen to the voice inside our self. We need to contemplate what we need to improve or change, keeping aware and protecting our self from those who suck our energy, because we live individually and have our own path to take. We are all responsible of our own happiness, are all created unique from every one else. About time to step out from the dark shadow of our life and live happily with peace and loved ones.

ABOUT THE IMAGE:

It is my son standing near the door, facing outside from my bedroom with the light on. The best spot to reflect his shadow on the wall. I shot this image to represent the soul from the dark shadow. To emphasise what is the message that poetry wants to give and to understand the deep meaning of the poem. This show is to remind us that sometimes we often forgot the best person that we need to look up to…. None other than… "OURSELF".

"I'M GLAD, I FOUND YOU"

by: Gemma Escolano

I've been searching for you all seasons of time
Every single day, I was looking for you
From the hot Summer days
Until to the frost chills of Winter months

From the Autumn of falling leaves
Until the Spring of flower's blossoms
Blooming everywhere, in the garden of dreams
Still searching you, but no trace of you

From the block of ice of Winter fall
Until it melts from hot Summer days
Turn into water, back to the river flow
Still missing you, but nowhere to be found

From the big smile of a giant sunrise
Slowly rising from behind the mountain of hope
Until it is kissing the sea of a silent night
Still looking for you, but no shadows of you

From the queue of the Facebook page
Until the chapter of chaos Instagram
Finally, I found you, hiding from your comfort zone
My searching was over, I'm glad I found you

Here I am now, talking to you with delightful heart
Finding you after long longing search
Even if our distance is quite far, even if I can't touch you
You touch my soul, with joyful in my heart

My happiness that lies within you
Here you are with me, completely in my heart
But please promise me, be here with me always
Stay with me, live with me and love me always.

Jalan Jalan Photography & Poetry
Gemma Escolano

ARTIST STATEMENT

I'M GLAD I FOUND YOU

ABOUT THE POEM:

This poem is all about the guy who told me the story of his searching for someone….that deep inside he felt the longing of his heart. He continued searching and finally he found this lady on the other side of Earth, but unfortunately this lady was already married and there's no way for them to be together. Though he promised whatever happens, he is always on her side to help her in anything and to love her, because he wants her to be happy.

ABOUT THE IMAGE:

It is me in this image shot by my daughter one Saturday of September early spring of 2019, the same time when we shoot the image for the book cover. It was a bit windy and the Sun was soothing and bright, it was a beautiful day. I'm holding my red hat to avoid the wind blowing it from me. My hair is almost covering my face, but I enjoyed that moment. The background behind me is the Opera House, the icon of Australia. Heaps of people around the area that are having jalan-jalan.

"LOVE IS PATIENT, LOVE IS KIND"

by: Kiana Escolano Yabut

I reminisce about our joyful times
The chemistry we had is left behind
Your sweet taste often wonders my mind
Of the day when you become a part of mine

My heart boils with pain
Cause, I never wanted you to leave me again
My life will never be the same
Unless you come back so I'm entertained

"Love is patient, love is kind", they say
But why must I have to pay?
Our love should be unconditional
Fruitful and be obtainable

However, that's impossible to reach
Due to your brand always being on a leash
But never mind that, my eyes are set on you
Although, at the end of the day I'll have let it through

Chocolate, chocolate
You'll always be my favourite
So wait for me, I'm always here
Or else my eyes will shed a tear.

Jalan Jalan Photography & Poetry
Gemma Escolano

ARTIST STATEMENT

LOVE IS PATIENT, LOVE IS KIND

ABOUT THE POEM:

The writer of this poetry is the girl of my life. An adorable, sweet lovely young lady. Her sense of writing a poem of love was so meaningful even though she compared it not to chocolate, but the essence of love beneath the sweetness of chocolate. Love is addictive and irresistible, so be mindful whom you offer your love. If the receiver of your love is deserving, it will bloom the sweetness and the magic of love normally, come back to you equally as true love. If this is true feelings or only infatuation, because of the superficial sweetness of taste, will only manifest later on. The sweetness of love if it's not real, will turn into a bitter dark chocolate.

ABOUT THE IMAGE:

It was a lovely day early April of 2019. Me and my two (2) friends from University (New Castle University, Australia) where I did my course of Nursing, were having girls out time. We ended up at these lovely Eden Gardens located in Macquarie Park, Macquarie NSW Australia. This place is huge and has lots of fun things to do, playground for the kids, a place that can cater a wedding garden, a friendly coffee shop, nursery where you can buy varieties of plants and a souvenir shop. You can see different kinds of lovely and vividly coloured flowers, sculptures shaped by creative minds from things that you can't imagine can create an interesting subject. This big and tall vases made of stone clay are taller than me. On top of this, a water fountain constantly flowing and dripping to the ground.

"FIRST THING LASTS"

by: Sean Arielle Turano Bondad

You're the first thing that appears in my mind
Secretly staring every time you're passing by
Couldn't think straight when you look into my eye
And yes I admit I'm still euphoric by your side

Life was just like a sheet of paper, till you started to write
One day you uttered my name, your hand made my veins hum wild
The sharpness, warmness, sweet gazing from your eyes
It's beyond words itself, just impossible to define

But why, does my world tell me that misery is what it gains
That though it now it seems endless, later unbearable pain prevails
I know it was to fortify, but it enfeebles me instead
Horrified from that fact, I chose to get you off my head

Life since then was bitter, life was really rough
It can never be better, it can never be enough
I never should have listened to what that cruel world said
I should've fought for you, now my chances are forfeited

All this time, I was wrong, believing that you won't stay at all
Surprised and unaware that you're actually there
Secretly gaze from far away
And that long time has proven how you really care

From then on, I know I owe you a fight
To face the world, who's against us reuniting
But instead of fighting, you taught me to surrender
And that surrender amazingly, pulled all ties together

The first and last thing that appears, in my mind was you
I'm glad is not a secret to stare and you're doing the same too
You still have that magical effect, when you look at me in the eye
My love, I'll say "Yes" just stay forever by my side

My life was a sheet of paper 'till you started to write
You have written the best things you've given me the sky
Though leaving you had hurt, you just don't get tired of trying
Now that we're together, there's surely no goodbye.

Jalan Jalan Photography & Poetry
Gemma Escolano

ARTIST STATEMENT

FIRST THING LASTS

ABOUT THE POEM:

The lovely story poem written by my niece is wonderful. The writer is an adorable, talented, sweet and lovely young lady. The feelings of love that comes up from this poetry is so intense with sadness and long waiting at the beginning, but it will turn out wonderful at the end. Better to wait and fight silently that everything turns out for the best. This poetry shows that by being patient in everything the magnificent reward will be yours at the end. All things that happen in our life, have a process to gain, to embrace and to enjoy. Acceptance of what is happening with open mind it gives light every step of the way.

ABOUT THE IMAGE:

This image of two (2) birds was magical. This represent the two lovers who are helping one another. If you look closer at this image, you can see the male bird holding in his beak the insect (their food) trying to feed the female bird. How wonderful to see this kind of creation, that even in the world of animals love is existing. I am enjoying taking photos of this place when I saw these lovely birds siting on the fence. I did not waste a single moment shooting this magical scene. I was amazed seeing them. It was the time of my birthday celebration, a week of holiday away from home early year of 2019. This image taken at Kangaroo Valley, South Coast of NSW Australia, two (2) hours drive from Sydney City and to Canberra ACT. Kangaroo Valley is the best tourist destination and one of the most beautiful areas in Australia.

"SEVEN PROMISES OF YOURS"

by: Aliyah Simoune Turano Bondad

In my hardest time, no one was around
In every struggle, that I was laying on the ground
You made me feel that I am not alone
"I'll be with you"
That's your promise that will be kept

No fears' coz no one can harm me
No tears 'coz no one can hurt me
No troubles 'coz no one can beat me
"I'll protect you"
That's your promise that will be kept

I am weak and I admit it
But you change it so I can do all things,
Because you gave me strength when you said,
"I'll be your strength"
That's your promise that will be kept

There's so many questions in my mind
But I trust you with all my heart
Because you're the answer from all the start
"I'll answer you"
That's your promise that will be kept

I don't need to worry for tomorrow
I don't need to worry forever
Because you are the great provider
"I'll provide for you"
That's your promise that will be kept

In this world full of sword, you are my shield
In my world full of darkness, you are my light
And your acceptance hugs me so tight
"I'll give you peace"
That's your promise that will be kept

I'm a sinner and you're a saviour
You love me no matter what
You crucified at the cross without any doubt
"I'll always love you"
That's your promise that forever will be kept.

ARTIST STATEMENT

SEVEN PROMISES OF YOURS

ABOUT THE POEM:

This poetry was written by my lovely and sweet niece. I was surprised at her creative mind of thinking. The way of her writing is precise and direct. The poem is all about the prayer. The strong belief and assurance of life, that when anything happens there is always help from above to resolve the problems, hurdles and troubles in life. There is no room for fear, anxiety and hopeless thinking, if coming from your heart you believe and have faith that you're not alone on your own journey in life. This prayer is the bright light to everyone, that guides those who are suffering from severe loneliness, pain, agony and downfall, who think there's no light coming their way. There is no exception, everyone of us can face this bumpy side of road, but at the end of the road the answer will come up….Just keep going and have faith in your heart.

ABOUT THE IMAGE:

I was thinking so many times of what was the image that suited to this poem? Then suddenly, came to my attention when I saw this figurine of angel on the top of my tall boy cabinet, as representative of a messenger from Heaven. I had this figurine of angel seven (7) years ago, it came from "The Milano Collection, Alabaster Art Sculpture" the Collector's Edition, was bought from a gift shop close to the City somewhere in Sydney. I set up my camera and arranged things to shoot. Placing a few flowers behind the angel added to the beauty of image. The background behind is my second pouring painting, as I love to paint as well. The colours of the painting are like Planet Earth. Thinking adding this to give more life of the image of The Angel behind the Earth.

"HEARTS"

by: John Yuri Andea

I fear that my heart fallible would tear
By love mistaken and sorrowful shame
For the clouds of tears that I can't bear
May break for uneventful day

Therefore, retribution evokes my mind
To lunatic actions done by heart
Heart with unending lustful sight
Until met by impulsion for home and heart

Though men be tough at sight
But inner soft and mind
Though men committed to a fight
But can be frail and be lost in a wild

Thus I fear that my fallible heart could tear
For the clouds of tears may break
That I can't take.

Jalan Jalan Photography & Poetry
Gemma Escolano

ARTIST STATEMENT

HEARTS

ABOUT THE POEM:

The writer of this poetry is one of my nephews. I was surprised the first time I heard from his mum that he also love writing poetry. I love his style of writing, the deepness and the words he used are synchronising to each other and the feelings are so intense. This poem is about the fallible heart, when it seems the feelings of love is real, but in the end it manifested the wrong feelings of love. Sometimes feelings are deceiving just because we can't see the core behind what we see is love. We can only recognise the superficial, that we believe this is real love, but it will end up in heartache, sadness and clouds of tears.

ABOUT THE IMAGE:

I took this image one afternoon in Spring time. I used the flower vase with flowers in it. Vase was made of capiz, one of my favourite materials made from Nature. Capiz is seashell originating from the place in Capiz Town, Visayan Region in Philippines. The background behind in this image was my first painting that is full of hearts with the colours of oranges, purples, yellows and greens. I used my painting of hearts to emphasise the poem about heart.

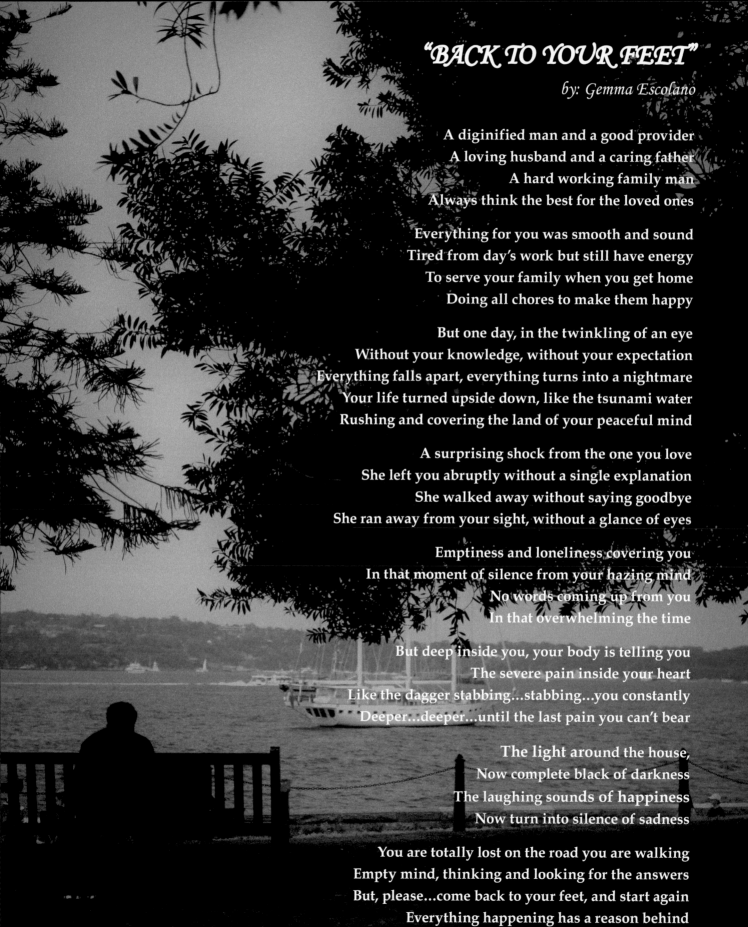

"BACK TO YOUR FEET"

by: Gemma Escolano

A diginified man and a good provider
A loving husband and a caring father
A hard working family man
Always think the best for the loved ones

Everything for you was smooth and sound
Tired from day's work but still have energy
To serve your family when you get home
Doing all chores to make them happy

But one day, in the twinkling of an eye
Without your knowledge, without your expectation
Everything falls apart, everything turns into a nightmare
Your life turned upside down, like the tsunami water
Rushing and covering the land of your peaceful mind

A surprising shock from the one you love
She left you abruptly without a single explanation
She walked away without saying goodbye
She ran away from your sight, without a glance of eyes

Emptiness and loneliness covering you
In that moment of silence from your hazing mind
No words coming up from you
In that overwhelming the time

But deep inside you, your body is telling you
The severe pain inside your heart
Like the dagger stabbing...stabbing...you constantly
Deeper...deeper...until the last pain you can't bear

The light around the house,
Now complete black of darkness
The laughing sounds of happiness
Now turn into silence of sadness

You are totally lost on the road you are walking
Empty mind, thinking and looking for the answers
But, please...come back to your feet, and start again
Everything happening has a reason behind

ARTIST STATEMENT

BACK TO YOUR FEET

ABOUT THE POEM:

This poem was written when I was in Taipei airport while waiting for my connecting flight going back home to Sydney. It was my short visit in Philippines, spending only two (2) weeks to attend an important event. This poem is dedicated to the person who is very close to my heart, like a big brother to me, a colleague, a mentor and a best friend. The sympathy I felt for his story was so intense and unforgettable. Sometimes in life, things happen that we can't do anything about, so we must embrace the process and let go of the pain.

ABOUT THE IMAGE:

It was a second weekend of December 2019 when I attended a business event in the City. My plan was to shoot a photo after the event as a background for this poetry. I went to the park near St. Mary Cathedral in Sydney, looking for something new as a subject to suit this poem, but had no luck there. I followed my instinct to go to Circular Quay, the heart of City, just to go around the Opera House. Walking a few miles away heading to Botanical Garden in the midday with the Sun above. I was enjoying taking photos of all the vivid flowers in that garden, but still in my mind wishing to catch a very good image for this poem. It was a tiring day, then I decided to go home. On my way back to train station, I was surprised to notice this man sitting alone on the bench under the tree facing the water, it was like magic. I can't get away on this site without pressing my shutter button on my camera. The image of what I've seen in my vision was perfectly manifested in front of my eyes. I was surprised and amazed for this wonderful moment that my wish was granted. The missing page of my book, now completely done.

"DRIFTING"

by: Blossoms Bloom

I have been drifting like a lifeless log
Not really caring, what goes in my surroundings
There are days when I stare at nothing
Sit and wonder why I feel empty yet believing?

That maybe you care for me
That maybe I am special
That you want to be with me
Just as I want to be with you.

I think restless thoughts, Mind wondering,
wanting to flee but where to?
I think with all my being, that there is someone
Somewhere, who will come whisk me away!

Make me happy, take me to a wonderful places
I have never been to, make me sway...
Swoon to his sweet embrace, soft whispering voice
Pronouncing his enduring love.

Eternal promise of a paradise-like existence
These and other blessings from above...
But where is he??

Jalan Jalan Photography & Poetry
Gemma Escolano

ARTIST STATEMENT

DRIFTING

ABOUT THE POEM:

This poem written by; Blossoms Bloom, is about the searching soul that continues waiting and hoping that one day the right love will come and rescue her from emptiness and sadness. Dreaming of wonderful place to live, sharing this with the love of her life. Majority of people when they reach the age of knowing, they felt something deep inside that they need to fill in. We continue searching for the answer, finding the missing page, looking the missing puzzle, and get the missing ingredients. Along the way we meet someone, it's like this is the one, but yet still have empty space in our existence. The missing half could be our Twin Flames, created when we are first moulded into one. At the right time these two will be reunited as one.

ABOUT THE IMAGE:

I love this photo, the rays of Sun's reflection from the water was magnificent, like a brilliant dust of gold spreading around. The timing was superb when I pressed the shatter button on my camera. The small wave created by a small boat passing through the river has given a dimension to the colours of this image that gives the body of water movement. Taken at Wiseman Ferry Park in Hawkesbury River, NSW Australia. This is a better place to unwind, relax stress free and feel the energy of Nature.

"THE RAIN LILY LADY"

by: Blossoms Bloom

There's a lady I know
She plants rain lilies row by row
Her rain lily lawn is magical
Her Facebook posts lyrical

I found her in a post on a gardener's group
Perched on a golden shower tree top
Golden yellow flowers adorned her head
Flowing blossoms like a precious crown

The tree was awesome
Long, long flowers cascading down
The lady perched on it was smiling enchantingly
She looked so happy, gloriously...

I was enthralled by the tree and the lady
She offered golden shower seeds for free
Amazed at her generosity and kindness
I sent her a friend request

Ma'am Alice, a lady I know
Thank you for accepting
I am grateful for your friendship
Your posts inspire and uplift

Your garden is an inspiration
It truly fuels my aspiration
For a lovely garden of my own
Wishing you more beautiful years
With your flowers, berries and all.

ARTIST STATEMENT

THE RAIN LILY LADY

ABOUT THE POEM:

This poetry is dedicated to a lady whom the writer (Blossoms Bloom) met online in social media. Because of the lady's friendly gesture and generosity, their friendship started to bloom. This time in our new generation, they say everything changes due to the computer world around the Globe. The people rapidly change, economic, status in life, the weather conditions and the atmosphere are evolving continuously. Whatever may change on this planet Earth, there's some people who are genuinely kind hearted, ready to help and to share whatever they have. They were not affected by massive changes of life every day. This could be a sign that this world heading towards a much more a better place to live.

ABOUT THE IMAGE:

The lovely garden of beautiful flowers beside Opera House, Sydney Australia, caught my attention to shoot this image. The light of the Sun radiates through these, makes these flowers attractive and illuminated.

"MY GRANDMA, VICTORIA"

by: Blossoms Bloom

I remember my grandma
Her name was Victoria
She passed away
At 100 + or so, they say

I recall meeting her in 2012
Still standing upright
But with very poor eyesight
She finally recognized me
Said, "How huge you have become, Bhe"

I smiled, gave her a hug
And 3 bills of 1k each in her bag
She took them, had a close peek
Waved her hands and put them to her cheek
Saying, "Yippee! Ang dami kong pera!!"

My grandma gave the most delicious massage
She taught me how to iron my blouse
Lent me funds for my passport
And her suitcase that travelled to many airports

My grandma....I remember
Her memories linger
In my heart, in my mind
We are intertwined.....

ARTIST STATEMENT

MY GRANDAMA VICTORIA

ABOUT THE POEM:

I love this poem about our grandma's name, Victoria. This poem written by one of my close relatives who also loves writing poetry. The details of her experiences during the time when our grandma was still alive is so touching. The happiness that she gave was priceless and meaningful. Simple happiness but quite memorable.

ABOUT THE IMAGE:

One morning around 7 o'clock in the middle of Winter time I woke up with a big surprise when I saw outside was full of fog everywhere. I can't easily see the surrounding, it's like huge smoke covering the whole place so even the Sun is hard to see. I ran quickly upstairs to grab my camera to take some photos of this. This image taken in front of our place. The subject is the grass with spider web hanging on it. The Sun was hardly seen and it's like a pale drawing of Sun attached to the sky.

"THOUGHTS OF YOU"

by: Kristine Olarita

Oftentimes I see myself blue
In a sea of troubles of the things I go through
But what matters most is who has been true
For she is tough, still trying to pursue her dreams

The dwindling feeling life had brought
Had me run in circles bringing doubts and distraught
For the epiphany of love I continue to seek
I prayed to God "May you not leave me weak"

Then you came and brought tranquillity into the waves
Gave me laughter and took me out of my cave
You made me better, stronger and brave
You're the missing peace, who uplifted me from the grave

Your love is sweet, mischievous and kind;
It is too vibrant – makes me feel blind
Now I wonder of what lingers in your mind?
For finally, the stars have aligned

As days went by, I thought of nothing but of how I was saved
From the dark shadows which had me enslaved
Of what pain and suffering could make you behave
You are a gift from the saving grace of our Devine
And now I am forever amazed.

ARTIST STATEMENT

THOUGHTS OF YOU

ABOUT THE POEM:

This poem was written by a young lady who is dear to me. Her type of writing in this poem about waiting for love is detailed and profound. You can feel the emotion added to it. The strong hope and wonder of her dreams becomes a reality, it's like a magic that saves her from loneliness.

ABOUT THE IMAGE:

One day in early March 2019, we went out having Jalan Jalan (going around and have fun). We ended up at this beautiful river of Wiseman Ferry Park, located on the Hawkesbury River, NSW Australia. The park is considered the Northern Gateway to the Shire. This place is excellent to have a family picnic, small party or gathering with friends and family. It was nearly sunset when we arrived at this place. The beautiful sunset slowly hiding behind the mountain is stunning and magnificent. The water on the river was so quiet and calming. I enjoyed pressing the shatter button on my camera so did not to miss out this golden colour of the Sun. The model in this image is the writer of this poetry.

ACKNOWLEDGEMENT

Writing a Poetry book has been a tougher journey than I thought, more valuable and satisfying than I could have imagined and a thing I thought could never have happened to me. This book could not be made without the support and love from my family, friends, and relatives.

First and for most, I give my humble, and grateful to our Almighty God for all the blessings that shower me throughout all my life. All the answers to prayers that have been granted to me in His time. He is the comfort of my heart and the guiding star that leads me into my journey of dreams. All I have are belonging to him.

To my mum, Linda, who gave me the courage to keep going with what I wanted to achieve in life despite everything that was blocking me along the way. Having her with me for most of the time of photography sessions, it becomes lighter on me because of her happy soul and always gets to go spirit. Her belief and tough personality have given me the strong foundation; that life is always beautiful with a loving, generous and sincere heart.

To my husband, Voltaire, who loves and helps me in every word put into my poetry with his humour and perseverance. To my children, Jayson, Vienne, Kevin, Kiana, and Reivie Jared, to my daughter-in-law, Rasha and to my grandson, Arden, you are all my jewels from my hidden box of memories, who believes and keep pushing me to attain my deepest desire of having my dreams to hold into my hands. I am so blessed to have you all in my life. Your love and inspiration gives me light for my darkest time of this journey.

Grateful to say to my dad, Gregorio G. Escolano and mommy Prime, who continue praying for me and are always reminding me of whatever we gain in life, we need to give thanks to God and share the blessing to others. To my sisters, Glenda and Pam, to my brothers, Eang and Gremer, to my brother-in-laws, Arnulfo and Bong, to my sister-in-law, Isay, to my nephews, Jemai, Micah and Quiel, thank you so much for all the love and prayers for me.

To my respectable bosses at work, Alan and Huntley, my deepest gratitude for all the support through all the years and trusting me that all things are possible with the works of an honest and sincere heart. To my lovely Managers, Rowena and Mary, for the love and understanding especially when I needed them most, you are there to comfort me with your warmth and hugs of security, always reminds me to look after myself before anything else, so I can give more love to others. To all my beautiful colleagues and friends at work, your cheerful and encouraging words are so beneficial, especially at time I felt weak and helpless. You are there for me to regain my strength and to continue my journey.

To all my friends and relatives around the world, pages are not enough to write all your names but you know who you are and all your names are written in my heart. My deepest and sincere gratitude for all your precious time, the love, continuity of support and belief in me that this book of poetry comes into the surface of reality.

The bunch of people behind the Balboa Publisher, who have a sincere heart and patience helping me through this odyssey of book to make my dream come into existence, from Senior Publishing Consultant: Joan Taylor; Publishing Consultant: Al Sampson; Publishing Service Associate: Rachel Abbey; Marketing Consultant: Pat Stone; Designer: Charisse Schelmer Hizon and to all the staff who are not mentioned that gives contribution and much effort to this book.

A very special thanks to Vincent Stead, who is the Editor of this book. Your generous help and understanding of where I came from, it means a lot for me. Without your sincere heart and with massive help, this dream of mine could not be possible.

My evermore grateful to my best friend, mentor, associate and like a big brother to me, Lito C. Uyan, who gave the big impact of fabulous prospective, brilliant ideas, great visions and excellent pieces of advice not only in the field of photography but also about the weaknesses in my life. He always reminds me to keep on track whatever bumpy road that I meet along the way. He is my strong wings beneath my dreams.

For all the Poets and Writers; Blossom Bloom, Kiana Escolano Yabut, Sean Arielle Turano Bondad, Aliyah Simoune Turano Bondad, John Yuri Andea, and Kristine Olarita, who contributed to this book of Poetry. My warmest gratitude for your time and efforts sharing the talent of your wonderful and creative minds.

Also my warm gratitude to all the wonderful people; Dr. Jeffrey Albert, Fred L. Isom, Dr. Michele Pascali, Dr. Alan C. E. Riley and Lito C. Uyan, who gave their awesome previews and trusted me to say their lovely thoughts with their sincere heart and precious time to help me with this book of poetry 'Vibrant Memories'.

It is my honour and pleasure having you all wonderful people being part of my journey that is a dream come into reality. Without your support and perseverance this dream won't become into surface. A dream from long time ago, now completely clear and bright. I am pleased to share to entire world my passion and my thoughts that can reach and touch their heart, to give hope and to give light. Even in the darkest time, there is small light that we can hold on. Follow your heart, follow your dream, never stop, and never surrender. Be yourself and be a shining star to each and everyone. This book, 'VIBRANT MEMORIES' is for you.

Gemma Escolano
Gemma Escolano Photos and Poetry,
JalanJalan Photography

GemmaEscolanopoetry

Gemma Escolano

Gemma Escolano Love Poem

Website: gemmaescolano.com
             JalanJalanphotographyandpoetry.com

Printed in the United States
By Bookmasters